# CRITICAL VIEWING OF TELEVISION

## A Book for Parents and Teachers

### Ibrahim M. Hefzallah, Ph.D.

UNIVERSITY
PRESS OF
AMERICA

LANHAM • NEW YORK • LONDON

Copyright © 1987 by

University Press of America,® Inc.

4720 Boston Way
Lanham, MD 20706

3 Henrietta Street
London WC2E 8LU England

Printed in the United States of America

British Cataloging in Publication Information Available

**Library of Congress Cataloging-in-Publication Data**

Hefzallah, Ibrahim M.
  Critical viewing of television.

  Includes index.
  1. Television broadcasting—Social aspects.
2. Television—Psychological aspects.  3. Television
programs—Evaluation.  4. Television audiences.
I. Title.
PN1992.6.H42  1987        302.2'345        86-32498
ISBN 0-8191-6107-1 (alk. paper)
ISBN 0-8191-6108-X (pbk. : alk. paper)

All University Press of America books are produced on acid-free
paper which exceeds the minimum standards set by the National
Historical Publication and Records Commission.

*To my family*

# ACKNOWLEDGMENTS

I owe a great deal of my expertise in critical analysis of media to two of my mentors at Ohio State University, Dr. I. Keith Tyler, and the late Dr. Edgar Dale.

I would like to acknowledge Fairfield University administration, faculty, and students for providing the intellectual climate that made the publication of this book possible. Teaching classes on critical viewing of television at Fairfield University, has helped me refine my treatment of the topic.

Also, I would like to acknowledge Westwood/Baywood the publisher of the *International Journal of Instructional Media* for granting me the permission to use some of my articles which appeared in the Journal and have special bearing on the topic of this book, and to reprint the article "Content Analysis of Television Commercials." This article was based on a comprehensive content analysis of television commercials conducted by my colleague Dr. W. Paul Maloney and myself. The article is included in Appendix I to illustrate to the reader the intricate structure of television commercials.

In addition, I would like to acknowledge the Advertising Research Foundation publisher of the *Journal of Advertising Research* for allowing me to use a section of the article "Are There Only Six Kinds of TV Commercials?" which was co-authored by Dr. W. Paul Maloney and myself, and appeared in Vol. 19, No. 4, 1979. This section is included in Chapter XI, Television Commercials.

While it is difficult to mention all the people who have directly or indirectly contributed to this publication, Mrs. Barbara Coe deserves particular credit for her patience in deciphering my handwriting, and for her professionalism in typing the manuscript.

Finally, to my family who had to put up with my long hours of work, and for their continuous encouragement, I don't have enough words to thank them.

# TABLE OF CONTENTS

# PREFACE

Critical viewers of television are capable of analyzing what they see and hear on television, distinguishing between reality and the world of television, making informed judgment and expressing thoughtful evaluation of programs watched, and making intelligent use of leisure time in which television viewing is one among other enjoyable activities.

Critical viewing of television is an outcome of planned activities in which understanding the medium of television and what it offers, and thinking about one's relationship with television are underlined. It is a skill that can and should be taught to the younger generation. However, before we can foster critical viewing in our children, we have to develop that skill and wholly believe in its necessity to provide our children with models of intelligent use of television. This book is written for parents and teachers.

# INTRODUCTION

Since television is watched by millions of children and young people for long hours every day, it is essential to develop their critical viewing abilities. Without discriminating parents and teachers, children will lack models of intelligent use of the television medium. The main objective of this book is to increase adults' understanding of television and to develop their critical viewing skills.

Based on the wealth of information on television and its effects, and on original research conducted by the author, comprehensive, yet easy-to-read material is presented.

The book contains three sections. The first section focuses on television as the most popular and intimate medium mankind has ever known. It stresses the public's need to stay in control of their television viewing.

The second section explores the persuasion and presentation techniques employed in television; the programming policy of television stations resulting in what we see on television; potential effects on the viewer of violence, sex, and commercials; and how television news can shape our understanding of the world.

Finally, the third section presents critical awareness exercises designed to increase the reader's awareness of his/her relationship to television and television methods of presentation and persuasion.

*"The critical-minded are active, not passive, in their reception of the printed and spoken word or the motion picture, television, and radio . . . They search out hidden assumptions, unwarranted inferences, false analogies. They are the good-natured skeptics and sometimes, unfortunately, the soured cynics . . . And they are our greatest hope for progress."*

*Edgar Dale*

1

# SECTION I

## INTRODUCTION

Television is watched by millions of people for long hours every day. It is the most popular medium of communication mankind has ever known.

Chapter I focuses on television's popularity, and Chapter II addresses the public's need to stay in command of their television experience.

CHAPTER I:  TV: THE POPULAR AND INTIMATE MEDIUM

CHAPTER II:  THE CRITICAL VEIWER

# Chapter I

# TV: THE POPULAR AND INTIMATE MEDIUM

*Never before in the history of communication has there been a medium as popular and intimate as TV - nor has there been a medium that captures the attention of millions of viewers for long viewing hours every day. New developments in telecommunications are expected to increase the popularity and the intimacy of the medium to the public. Developing the public's critical viewing skills ensures the intelligent use of the most popular medium of communication.*

## A POPULAR MEDIUM

TV has captured the attention of both the young and the old, the illiterate and the literate, the poor and the rich, the advertiser and the consumer, the politician and the public. It has become the focal point in many of our living rooms. Through it, its audience is entertained and informed. TV appeals to the imagination and fantasy of a large segment of its audience. Its culture is popular. (1) It relies heavily on programmatic ideas which the majority of people can identify. Its information messages (news programs, ads, etc.) are designed to be grasped and understood by a majority of its audience.

TV is in the business of selling the presence of an audience to the advertiser. (2,3) The more people watch a show, the more money can be obtained from selling advertising time. The decision to finance and operate television for maximum profits, supplied totally by advertising, has turned the medium into a market place. (4) To increase the size of the audience of a program, the program has to appeal and capture the interest of a large segment of the population.

The process of accessing information or an entertainment program on television is simple and easy. Turning on the TV set requires no skill. Operation of videotape machines for recording and playing back is not that complicated. Home video recorders are becoming more popular day by day. *The New York Times* (5) reported that the sales of video cassette recorders totaled 4.2 million units in 1983. This figure is twice that of 1982 (2.1 million units). Also, the sales of blank cassettes were 57 million units in 1983 vs. 24.7 million units in 1982. (5)

5

On January 17, 1984, the Supreme Court ruled (5-4) that the use of videorecorders to tape television programs at home does not violate copyright laws. (6,7) One could expect that more people will be using videocassette recorders to record programs off-the-air to watch at their own leisure and to develop their own videocassette libraries.

In 1981, the Congressional House Subcommittee approved guidelines for "Off-the-air Recording" of broadcast television programs for educational use. (8) These guidelines state that a broadcast program can be taped off-the-air for viewing in a classroom up to two times during the first ten consecutive school days following its recording. The tape can be kept for reference by the instructor up to the 45th day following the date of the broadcast, after which it should be erased. However, a long-term retention agreement is possible to obtain at a very reasonable fee. These guidelines encourage schools to use broadcast material to enrich classroom presentation. This will help make TV a more popular instructional medium.

Its promise to entertain and its easy accessibility helped make the rate at which TV invaded American homes faster than any other invention. The following table shows the speed at which TV and other modern inventions entered 80% of the American homes. (9)

| Invention | Years to enter 80% of the American homes |
|---|---|
| Telephone | 80 |
| Electricity | 62 |
| Cars | 49 |
| Electric washing machines | 47 |
| Refrigerators | 37 |
| Radio | 25 |
| TV | 10 |

Cable TV is a giant that was born out of the necessity to provide a clear signal to households which could not receive a clear signal by using home antennas. During its early years (1950-1970), cable's growth was very slow. In 1970, 7.5% of the nation's households were wired for cable. (10) During that time, the emphasis was put on providing clear signals to homes deprived of good reception due to distance from TV transmitters, or due to geographical obstruction to the broadcast signal. (11) By mid 1970's, two developments occurred which put cable growth on an accelerating curve. First was the introduction of satellite transmission which provides centralized cost-effective distribution of programs such as movies on movie channels. (11,p.127) This development invited large companies to enter the field of cable operation and production of software. At present, the cable industry contains various large corporations which own a number of cable systems throughout the U.S.

These companies, called "Multiple System Operators" (MSO), (10, pp. 4.13 4.14, 11, pp. 243-244) can benefit from the size of their operation by purchasing programs on a group basis, and by the availability of capital to help finance the construction and the expansion of their systems. Second, the Federal Communications Commission, (FCC) relaxed rules to allow cable companies to import distant signals. This led to the availability of more programs for the viewer to choose from. It also led to the emergence of the first superstation, WTBS in Atlanta. (11, p.112) The superstation transmits its signal via satellite to cable operators in other markets around the country. These developments increased the popularity of cable television. No longer is poor reception the reason for hooking to cable. Attractive alternative programming and other electronic services appeal to the public. By 1990, it is estimated that 54.9 million American homes will have cable service. (12)

The popularity of the medium is also reflected by the millions of people who watch TV. Special programs can attract close to 100 million viewers in the States alone. It is also reflected by the number of hours viewers spend in front of the TV. At present, TV occupies more time than any other medium. On the average, teens spend 23 hours/week watching TV, children 2-5 years spend 29 hours/week. (1, p.3; 13, pp. 183-184) It has been reported that children spend more time in front of the TV than they spend in regular schooling. (14) Based on viewing estimates and the frequency of television commercials, a person by the age of 65 years will have watched the equivalent of one and one-half years of TV commercials alone! Quite a popular medium!

Because of its popularity among people, advertisers find TV a gold mine. TV advertising grew from 300 million dollars in 1952 (2, p.43) to around 16 billion dollars in 1983. (15) Almost half a billion dollars a year are spent on children's advertising only. (14, p.96)

Capitalizing on TV invasion of homes, educators have sought to use it to educate the young and old. Studies on the use of television in education have proven that home-bound students welcome TV as an educational medium. (16) With growing emphasis on self-improvement through continuing education, the adult learner finds educational TV a friendly source of information and a convenient means of gaining college credits. (17-19)

In England, around 78,000 students are enrolled in the Open University. By 1980, 33,000 students graduated with a bachelor's degree. (20) Although education in the Open University implements the distant learning concept in which TV forms 10% of students' activities, yet that segment in course work is essential to the pacing of the student in the course and in helping the adult learner to identify with unseen colleagues who tune in for the programs.

Educational TV programs designed to be course components have attracted learners in the U.S. According to CPB study on the use of television in higher education, 32% of higher education institutions offered a total of 10,594 courses over television in 1984-85, an average of twelve courses per college. Those colleges enrolled 399,212 students in the television courses, an average of 38 per course and 442 TV enrollments per college. (21)

The success of telecourses is partially due to good quality TV educational material that attracts and sustains the interest of the adult learner. Prior to the creation of the Corporation for Public Broadcasting (CPB) (1967) and of the Public Broadcasting Service (PBS) (1969), the use of television in education was a mixture of success, frustration, and failure. In many instances, the design of educational programs was poor. Many programs featured talking heads and televising a classroom practice. With the adoption of a system approach in teaching, TV is now treated as an intricate component in a teaching/learning system. Adopting this approach freed the educational TV designer from "televising a course." The emphasis shifted instead to "designing an interesting course" in which print, TV, non-print media, as well as student/instructor consultations are explicitly indicated. By 1974, a "new breed" of telecourse producers had emerged. Several institutions began producing telecourses that were educationally sound and visually more exciting than earlier educational TV material. Some of the new producers and telecourse designers are: Miami-Dade Community College District, Coast Community College, Southern California Consortium, and University of Mid-America.

During the fall season of 1984, PBS made seven telecourses available to public broadcasting stations. (22) According to PBS, 34% of the population between the age of 18 and 45 (31,000,000) who were not in college in 1981, said that they would like to take a college course via television and that they would be willing to pay for it. (23)

With the rapid technological developments in microprocessors, telecommunications and visual recording and retrieving, learning at home via the TV screen will become even more popular. Future uses of telecourses will increase through the availability of alternative delivery systems. (24) Integrating microcomputers with video playback units such as videodisc helps the production of individualized learning packages for home as well as school use. Special training packages will be produced to cover a variety of fields, which one could use in the privacy of his/her home.

In addition, the abundance of channels on cable TV makes it possible to reach a "non-mass" audience to educate or train. Technological advances continue so rapidly. The introduction of Teletext, information banks, and other applications of computer-video retrieval systems will increase the popularity of an already popular medium.

## A CLOSE AND INTIMATE MEDIUM

People have developed strong close relationships with TV. Television is a welcomed guest that keeps people company in their privacy. A television set is usually placed where it can be easily seen and comfortably watched. Accordingly, it occupies a prominent place in living rooms, family rooms, playrooms, bedrooms, and even in the kitchen.

The atmosphere of watching television is leisurely and cozy. People enjoy the comfort, informality, and warmth of their homes while watching television. In a recent report on leisure in America, it was reported that Americans prefer to spend their leisure time at home, and that television viewing leads the list of preferred leisure activities at home. (1)

With the advancement of electronics, TV sets will be more portable and more efficient and still at an affordable price to many. TV sets in the size of wrist-watches are in their early days of being introduced to the public. However, they symbolize the successful miniaturization of television sets. Miniaturization of TV sets will make it easier to carry and operate the television set almost anywhere one desires. This in turn will make people become closer to their television sets. That closeness will foster more dependability on television for passing time and receiving information. At present, TV is the most used entertainment medium of communications by Americans. Moreover, 65% of U.S. adults rely on TV as their principal source of information. (25) The dependence on the TV set to display information is also expected to increase with the development of information utilities which can be accessed from home through cable connections or telephone lines and a microcomputer keyboard.

Closeness and intimacy to TV are reinforced by its content and presentation techniques. TV presents a variety of material to entertain, to educate, to inform, and to sell a product. Both the content and the presentation techniques attract and capture the attention of the masses. Two elements of content and presentation techniques have a significant impact on making TV not only an attention-capturing medium, but also an intimate medium. These elements are: intimate content, and close-up and subjective angle shots.

## *Intimate Content*

The intimate television content ranges from presenting people in intimate and private life situations to advertising intimate products. TV leads us behind the walls of a prison to make us vicariously experience the agony of its inhabitants. It takes us in the living-room of a family to witness an argument between two spouses experiencing marital problems. Through TV we learn about the intimate life of leaders, politicians, scientists, ordinary people, criminals, policemen, prostitutes, homosexuals, etc. It presents to us delicate problems that we might find ourselves shy to address with our own children. TV commercials address many intimate topics from problems of bad breath to efficient feminine napkins. Some commercials capitalize on our fears of not being socially acceptable and point out ways of overcoming those fears. Repeating such messages over and over again, TV keeps on addressing very intimate topics that a person might not share with a close friend. Applying the "you" approach, it seems to the viewer as if the broadcaster, or the advertiser, is directing his message to the individual viewer.

9

## Close-up and Subjective Angle Shots

Due to the relatively small size of the TV screen, the TV maker relies heavily on close-up shots and ultra close-up shots of performers. Watching the performers from a very close distance, we come to recognize TV stars, newscasters, and masters of ceremonies as people we know.

To depict a scene or shot from the performer's point of view, subjective angle shots are used. In these shots, the viewer is placed in the position of the performer as the camera reveals to the viewer what the performer is visually experiencing in the scene. This technique tends to increase the viewers' interaction with the events of the program and reinforces his/her identification with the performer.

Using close-up and subjective angle shots to present soap-opera characters, for instance, in their daily life tragedies, hopes, and dilemmas helps establish those characters as personal acquaintences of some soap-opera fans. In talk shows, a similar relationship is usually established between the master of ceremonies and the viewer. Donald Horton and Richard Wohl called this relationship a "para-social relationship." (26) It is so called because the relationship is "based upon an implicit agreement between the performer and viewer that they will pretend the relationship is not mediated — and that it will be carried on as though it were a face-to-face encounter." (26) Horton and Wohl explained the conditions of the response to the performer in parasocial relationship as "analagous to those in primary groups. The most remote and illustrious men are met as if they were in the circle of one's peers." (26) According to Horton and Wohl, the same conditions are true of a character in a story who comes to life on the television screen. For the great majority of the television audience, the para-social relationship established between the audience, and television performers and master of ceremonies affects one's social understanding. As Horton and Wohl put it, "It (para-social relationship) provides a social milieu in which everyday assumptions and understandings of primary group interaction and sociability are demonstrated and reaffirmed." (26)

Never before in the history of communications has there been a medium as popular and intimate as TV. Nor has there been a medium that captures the attention of millions of viewers for long viewing hours every day. Such a medium should be studied and examined by viewers. Developing the public's critical viewing skills, especially that of young people, helps ensure intelligent use of the TV medium. This can be achieved through formal critical viewing skills curricula in schools (see Chapter XIV), informal discussion of television at home, and by parents setting up intelligent examples for television viewing for their children. The abundance of television channels and programs through cable, satellite, and video recording technology makes it more pertinent these days to develop audiences', especially young people's, television discriminating abilities. As Marie Winn put it, "We must learn to control TV so it does not control us." (27)

# REFERENCES

1.  Van Dyck, Nicholas B., "Families & Television," *Television & Children*, Summer 1983, pp. 3-11.

2.  Leibert, Diane E., "Television Advertising and Values," Ben Logan (Ed.), *Television Awareness Training, The Viewer's Guide for Family & Community*, Abingdon/Nashville, 1979.

3.  Primeau, Ronald, *The Rhetoric of Television*, Longman, Inc., 1979, p. 102.

4.  Greenfield, Jeff, *Television: The First Fifty Years*, New York: Crescent Books, 1982, pp. 153-154.

5.  *The New York Times*, Sunday, 1/22/84, Sec. 4, p. 1.

6.  Sony Corporation of America vs. Universal City Studios, N. 81-1687, *U.S. Law Week*, Jan. 17, 1984.

7.  For more information on the issue, refer to: Paul S. Wallace, Jr., "Copyright Law: Legalizing Home Taping of Audio and Video Recordings," Issue Brief Number IB82075, The Library of Congressional Research Service, Major Issues System.

8.  *Congressional Record*, Oct. 14, 1981.

9.  Schramm, Wilbur, *Responsibilities in Mass Communications*, New York: Harper & Brothers, 1957, p. 23.

10. Robb, Scott, *Television/Radio Age Communications Coursebook*, Englewood Cliffs, New Jersey: Communications Research Institute, 1978-79 edition, pp. 4-20.

11. Baldwin, Thomas F. and D. Stevens McVoy, *Cable Communication*, Prentice-Hall, 1983, p. 9.

12. U.S. Department of Commerce, Bureau of the Census, *Statistical Abstract of the United States*, 1986, p. 248.

13. Cole, Barry, (ed.), *Television Today: A Close-Up View, Readings from TV Guide*, New York: Triangle Publications, Inc., 1981, pp. 183-184.

14. Kaye, Evelyn, *The ACT Guide to Children's Television or . . . How to Treat TV with T.L.C.,* Revised Edition, Boston: Beacon Press, 1979, pp. 3-5.

15. *Advertising Age,* Volume 55, No. 1, January 2, 1984, p. 13.

16. Chu, Godwin C. & Wilbur Schramm, *Learning from Television: What the Research Says,* NAEB, 1967.

17. Randolf, Deborah A., "Colleges Offer More Courses Through TV," *The Wall Street Journal,* Nov. 20, 1980.

18. National University Consortium for Telecommunications in Teaching, University of Maryland University College, MD. Videotape featuring students' comments on directed study.

19. Community Junior Colleges *Extravaganza* (videotape).

20. BBC, *The BBC and the Open University,* 1980.

21. CPB, "A National Study of the Educational Uses of Telecommunications Technology in America's Colleges and Universities" (Survey Year 1984-85), *Research Notes,* September, 1986, No. 1, Washington D. C.

22. PBS Adult Learning Service, "Television Information Packet for the Summer and Fall, 1984, Adult Learning Schedules."

23. PBS, PTV-3 Adult Learning Programming Department, "A Background Paper for the Feb. 26, 1982 Teleconference on the Partnership between Public TV and Higher Education to Deliver Adult Learning Courses," p.16.

24. Munshi, Kiki Skagen, *Telecourses: Reflections '80,* CPB. Washington D.C., 1980, p. 63.

25. Brown, Les, *The New York Times Encyclopedia of TV*, Times Books, 1977, p. 303.

26. Horton, Donald and R. Richard Wohl, "Mass Communications and Para-Social Interaction: Observation on Intimacy at a Distance," *Journal of Psychiatry,* Vol. 19, No. 3, August, 1956.

27. Winn, Marie, *The Plug-In Drug,* New York: The Viking Press, 1977.

# Chapter II

## THE CRITICAL VIEWER

*Without an audience, television doesn't exist. With passive audience, anything can go on television. With a critical audience, only good television material can continue to exist.*
*Therefore, the goal of developing audience critical viewing skills is twofold:*
   *1. to ensure and maximize the positive effects of television, and*
   *2. to improve the overall quality of television programs to meet the standards of the critical viewer.*

## THE NEED TO DEVELOP CHILDREN'S CRITICAL VIEWING ABILITIES

In the early thirties, the power of motion pictures and their effects on youth were recognized. Based on the intensive and comprehensive Payne Fund Studies conducted at Ohio State University, 1930-1933, a textbook, *How to Appreciate Motion Pictures,* focusing on teaching motion pictures discrimination was published in 1935. (1) "The intent was to teach the adolescent how to judge pictures for himself by setting standards, and to teach him how to apply them. It was believed that a discriminating audience would be a constructive power for control of what would be produced." (2)

More recently, in 1969, Dale the author of the above-mentioned book explained the difference between a critical-minded and a sponge-minded person. He said:

The "sponge"-minded absorb with equal gullibility what they see at the movies, what they read in the newspapers, what they hear over television and radio. They are the passive viewers, readers, listeners. Fair game for advertisers, they spend huge sums for patent medicines each year. Even in their student days, they accepted without a flicker of distrust what the textbook said or what they heard from the lecture platform. Porous as sponges, their minds absorb for a brief time but do not assimilate.

The "critical"-minded are active, not passive, in their reception of the printed and spoken word or the motion picture, television, and radio. They constantly ask: "Is it true? Where's your evidence?" and "What do you mean by 'true'?" They search out hidden assumptions, unwarranted inferences, false analogies. They are the good-natured skeptics and sometimes, unfortunately, the soured cynics. They give the ill-informed and inaccurate teacher many a bad moment. And they are our greatest hope for progress. (3)

Schools teach critical skills in literature. They still fail, however, to see that television is a new form of today's children's literature, a form that they usually spend more time with than the written literature format. Children become regular users of television at an early age. For an average child, the number of hours spent watching television from age 3 to age 18 years exceeds the total number of hours spent in regular schooling. Most of those hours are spent in watching programs that will not help make children better able to cope with life. Research on the effects of the medium of television on children "...increasingly demonstrates that television's overall impact on children is a topic that cannot be dismissed lightly." (4) Although television occupies a large percentage of the child's active time, yet ". . . it (television) has been relatively free of the legal and moral constraint that are imposed on other institutions in their dealings with children." (4)

Children are a special audience with special needs. Unfortunately, children are served less well by television than any other significant audience. Educators recognize the need for programming that will enrich children's lives and broaden their ability to select the most appropriate programs. Children, like anybody else decide to view television first, and then select the most acceptable or least objectionable of available programs. (5) To minimize the negative effects of television on children, it becomes necessary to develop the child's television discriminating ability.

This can be achieved through formal critical viewing skills curricula in schools (see Chapter XIV), informal discussion of television at home, and *most important by adults setting up models of intelligent viewing of television.*

## THE NEED TO DEVELOP ADULTS' CRITICAL VIEWING SKILLS

To help our children to use television in an intelligent manner, we ourselves have to use it in an intelligent manner. Before we can foster taste in our children, we have to develop that taste ourselves and wholly believe in its necessity. (3, p.380) This entails developing adults' television discriminating abilities, and an awareness of the role of television as a mass medium in the society.

Adults should realize that as viewers they are "...full participants in the television system, as responsible as the industry itself for how things are, and in a better position to break free and cause change than is any other part of the system." (6) "They need to be fully aware that decisions in the television industry are economic decisions and that we are kidding ourselves into a dangerous apathy if we think television is a carefully controlled medium where some mythical 'they' look out for our interest." (6) Adults need to develop the attitude that "the consumer is in part responsible for the quality of films, television, and radio. Every time we tune in a program, buy a ticket to a movie theater, we are voting for the continuance of that kind of program." (3, p. 420)

Without an audience television does not exist. Accordingly, we share the responsibility with the television industry in both the bad and good about television programs, and there is no way of avoiding the challenge of becoming critical viewers and intelligent consumers of television programs.

## THE CRITICAL VIEWER

To be a critical viewer is to stay in control of one's television viewing. This skill is an outcome of developing a clear understanding of the television medium, and of thinking about our relationship with television.

The relationship that each one of us has with television is personal. First, we differ in how television affects us. Effects of television on viewers are a result of a dynamic process in which the viewer and the television content interact. Since viewers are different from one another, the same television content can evoke different responses from different viewers.

Second, we differ in what each one of us likes to watch and for what purpose. Basically, we can identify three groups of viewers. First, there is a group of viewers who watch television just to pass the time.

The second group of viewers has carefully thought about the place of television in their lives, and developed viewing guidelines for themselves and for their dependents. The third group is composed of those who seldom watch television, especially commercial entertaining programs, and to their surprise find themselves living in the midst of a television culture.

Regardless of the group that one belongs to, or how television affects us, critical viewing is a skill needed by all.

Critical viewers of television are capable of:

(a) analyzing what they see and hear on television;
(b) distinguishing between reality and the world of television;
(c) making informed judgments and expressing a thoughtful evaluation of programs they watch; and
(d) making intelligent use of their leisure time in which television viewing is one among other enjoyable activities.

Critical viewing comes from within. It is not imposed. It is an outcome of planned activities in which understanding the medium of television and what it offers, and thinking about one's relationship with television are underlined. It is a skill that can and should be taught.

There are those who believe that thinking about television spoils the fun that one might get from watching television. "After all," they say, "you watch television to relax and not to think, especially after a hard day of work."

15

Contrary to this claim, critical viewing increases one's enjoyment of television. First, critical viewers are more selective in what they watch than the average viewer, and thus avoid being frustrated by poor quality and mediocre programs.

Second, understanding the medium of television can help reveal to the critical viewer intricate aspects of television programs which remain unnoticed by the average viewer. This makes television watching an interesting experience.

Third, knowing the difficult task of producing good television material, a critical viewer usually enjoys and appreciates quality programs more than the average viewer.

----

To summarize, based on the degree of modern society's dependence on television for information, entertainment, and for spending a large portion of leisure time, as well as on the basis of the tremendous effects that television has on every one of us, developing critical viewing skills should not be left to chance. Planned learning strategies for developing young people's critical viewing skills are a must in school curricula. Prerequisite to the implementation of such curricula is the development of the adults' (teachers' and parents') ability to interact intelligently with television, and to practice critical viewing skills.

This book is written for the adult learner, parents, and teachers. SECTION II, Understanding the Television Experience, explores the persuasion and presentation techniques employed in television; the programming policy of television stations resulting in what we see on television; potential effects on the viewer of violence, sex, and commercials; and how television news can shape our understanding of the world we live in.

SECTION III, On Becoming A Critical Viewer, presents critical awareness exercises designed to increase the reader's awareness of his/her relationship to television and television methods of presentation and persuasion; and reviews nationally published school critical viewing curricula to help parents and teachers in advocating and selecting suitable critical viewing curricula for their youngsters.

# REFERENCES

1.  Dale, Edgar, *How to Appreciate Motion Pictures,* New York: The MacMillan Company, 1935.

2.  Charters, W.W., *Motion Pictures and Youth: A Summary,* New York: The MacMillan Company, 1935, p.59.

3.  Dale, Edgar, *Audio-Visual Methods of Teaching,* 3rd edition, The Dryden Press, 1969, p. 418.

4.  Melody, William, *Children's Television: Economics of Exploitation,* New Haven: Yale University Press, 1973, p. 85.

5.  Comstock, George, "The Teen Age Audience: Looking for Answers," *Television and Children,* Fall 1982, p. 65.

6.  Logan, Ben, "Television: Introduction and Overview, They Started the Revolution Without Me," *Television Awareness Training, the Viewer's Guide for Family and Community,* Ben Logan (ed.), Abingdon/Nashville, 1979, p. 9.

# SECTION  II

# PART I

## THE TELEVISION MEDIUM

A critical viewer needs to understand the medium of television. Television is a unique form of communication. PART ONE examines the language of television, its similarities and differences from other forms of communication; the visual and audio elements in television communication; and the syntax and style of the unique language of television.

# Chapter III

# THE TELEVISION LANGUAGE

*Human beings are capable of communication with each other. Over the centuries, symbolic systems or languages have been developed and perfected to maximize the efficiency of human communication.*

*Television "talks" to us in a unique language. A critical viewer of television needs to understand the basics of this language, and its techniques of evoking audience's response.*

*This chapter briefly examines the television language.*

## WHAT IS LANGUAGE?

The concept of language is not confined to audible noises or visible characters and symbols. Some scholars recognize that pictures have a language of their own. Floyde Brooker believes that verbal language is only one of the many ways of conveying a message. In his article "Communication in the Modern World" (in *Audio Visual Materials of Instruction*, the Forty-Eighth Yearbook of the National Society for the Study of Education, part 1), he explains this idea:

> In the course of history, man has used almost everything in his environment, and almost every power of his physical being, as a vehicle to carry his messages and to receive messages from others. He grunted his way to phonetic speech, fingered and daubed his way to art, used his muscles to develop many forms of the dance, and learned to give meaning by the pitch of his voice and by the way he used the muscles of his face. He gathered pieces of sticks and laid them in his track, blazed trees to tell others of the path, used the smoke of his campfire to carry his messages, used his hands to talk with strangers, developed rituals to tell the story of the tribe; and, finally, like Prometheus, reached into the clouds to make his messages ride the lightning. (1)

"Every individual," Brooker continues, "needs and uses more than one language. No language ever duplicates another, for each language is an art

21

form and exists only because it can express an area of experience better than other languages can."

Television has its own language. To create it, the video scriptwriter integrates four media: 1) verbal language, 2) pictures, 3) music, and 4) sound effects. He/she must, however, think primarily in terms of pictures since the visual part is the prime element in video communication. The ideas expressed in the script's written language are recast in terms of moving pictures, dialogue, music, and sound effects.

## THE LINGUISTICS OF VIDEO

Languages, both verbal and non-verbal, are of two major types, discursive and non-discursive. A discursive (successive) language, such as the verbal language, has basic units (words), and a syntax (grammatical rules) for arranging the basic units to convey the intended meaning. A non-discursive language, such as a still picture, presents all of its communicative elements simultaneously. (2)

*The verbal language* is the oldest and the most commonly used discursive communication medium. Its basic units are the words. Meaning is conveyed by arranging the words successively, according to the grammatical rules. If we change the sequence of the words, we change the meaning. For example, if we interchange the place of the first and last word in the sentence "Johnny hit the ball" to read "The ball hit Johnny," we have changed the meaning completely.

To illustrate the discursiveness of the television language, let us imagine a simple sequence constructed from three shots.

Shot 1 - Mr. Y. sitting behind his desk smiling
Shot 2 - Mr. X. at the office door of Mr. Y. He is holding a gun
Shot 3 - Mr. Y's expressionless face

The possible interpretation of this sequence could be "Mr. Y. is facing a serious situation."

If we interchange shot 1 and shot 3, we get the following sequence:

Shot 1 - Mr. Y's expressionless face
Shot 2 - Mr. X. at the office door of Mr. Y. He is holding a gun.
Shot 3 - Mr. Y. sitting behind his desk smiling

The possible interpretation of this sequence could be "Mr. Y. is not facing a serious situation - or, at least, he is not frightened."

The discursiveness of the language of moving images has been recognized since the dawn of film making. Two salient characteristics of discursive languages were experimented with during the era of silent motion pictures. These characteristics were: (1) a specific meaning of a shot depends on its

22

place within a sequence of shots, and (2) a sequence of shots can depict a meaning that is not inherent to any of the individual shots forming that sequence. As early as 1919, those characteristics were demonstrated. (3) In one experiment three sequences were composed using a close-up shot of an actor's face in composure, and close-up shots of a bowl of soup, a dead lady in a coffin, and a little girl playing with her Teddy bear. The three sequences were edited as follows:

| Sequence #1 | Sequence #2 | Sequence #3 |
|---|---|---|
| close-up of an actor | close-up of an actor | close-up of an actor |
| bowl of soup | dead lady | baby girl |
| close-up of an actor | close-up of an actor | close-up of an actor |

An audience, unaware of the sequences structure marveled at the ability of the actor to show the heavy pensiveness of this mood over the forgotten soup, his sadness toward the dead lady, and his fatherly attitude toward the baby girl. Since the shot of the actor was exactly the same shot in the three sequences, the experiment showed that (1) a single shot (basic unit) does not have a specific meaning, (2) the meaning of the shot depends on its place within the sequence and (3) a sequence of shots can depict a meaning that is not inherent to any of its basic units.

## The Basic Units of The TV Language

The basic units of the television language are shots. From shots having pictorial unity, sequences are formed. A sequence is an episodic portion of a program characterized by an inherent unity. From different sequences, the program is built. Therefore, at the foundation of the TV program structure is the shot. In this sense shots are compared with words in the verbal language. The shot is composed from four elements: the picture, verbal language, music, and sound effects. Those four elements interact to reinforce their effectiveness in communicating the intended meaning of a shot. In structuring the shot from its components, the TV producer/director attempts to remove any insignificant element within those components that might distract the viewer, and integrate the selected elements to form the basic unit of the television program.

In forming a shot, attention has to be given to three other factors: (a) the duration of the shot, (b) its place in a sequence of shots, and in the whole program, and (c) the transition from both the preceding and succeeding shots. Those three factors form basic syntax and style considerations.

## The TV Language Syntax

The TV language syntax is defined as the rules for structuring a sequence

23

from a series of shots, and the program from a series of sequences.

Shots as well as sequences may be joined together by optical effects such as fades, dissolves, and wipes, or simply by cutting from one shot to the other and from one sequence to another. These transition techniques help establish program continuity. They also help communicate meanings not necessarily expressed in the shot. For instance, the use of a dissolve to denote passage of time or the birth of an idea from another, and the use of fading-in and fading-out to show actors' subjective perception, and the use of a wipe to represent simultaneous action. Moreover, juxtaposing of contrasting shots or sequences through cutting can generate ideas in the mind of viewers which were not expressed in the separate shots or sequences. (HBO, *Not Necessarily the News* applies this principle in structuring the show.)

## *The Style of the TV Language - Editing*

Editing, the style of the TV language, is the art of putting the program together shot by shot and sequence by sequence. There are two aspects in editing: physical editing and creative editing. By physical editing is meant all the technical steps followed in the process of editing. Creative editing means the artistic selection of the best shots that affect the audience. Artistic editing offers the television maker the ability to manipulate time, space and even reason, yet still remain credible. It is what makes a mechanical prop a frightening shark in *Jaws* and human beings reduced to the size of microscopic organisms in *The Fantastic Voyage*.

In the following two chapters, the visual and the audio elements of the basic unit of the television language will be discussed, followed by a chapter on the syntax and the style of television.

Television "talks" to us in a unique way. A critical viewer of television needs to understand the basics of the television language, and its techniques of evoking audience's response.

# REFERENCES

1. Brooker, F.E., "Communication in the Modern World," in *Audio-Visual Materials of Instruction.* Forty-Eighth Yearbook, Part I, NSSE, 1949.

2. Hefzallah, I.M., "A Linguistic Definition of Communication Media,"*International Journal of Instructional Media,* Volume 3 (3), 1975-76. pp.243-253.

3. V.I. Pudovkin, *Film Technique and Film Acting,* New York: Grove Press, Inc., 1976.

# Chapter IV

## THE VISUAL ELEMENT
## OF TELEVISION

*The basic unit of the television language is the shot. The shot is composed primarily from two elements: the visual, and the audio elements. This chapter focuses on the visual element of television.*

*Television is primarily a visual medium. The principle of relying on the picture element in television and motion pictures communication is known as the "Principle of Visual Primacy."*

*In the early days of motion pictures, the forerunner of television, filmmakers emphasized duplicating real things and events. Later, the strength of film communication was realized to be in the ability of the camera to manipulate reality to achieve expressive images. Also, it was realized that the visual element in television and films can do more than represent or interpret reality. It can imply messages.*

*Prerequisite to critical viewing of television is the understanding of the visual element of television and its implying power.*

## THE PRINCIPLE OF VISUAL PRIMACY

When a person tunes in, he/she expects to see something. When the screen fades in, the spectator anticipates an action about to unfold.

A skilled TV program-maker thinks in terms of pictures that move. The principle of reliance on the picture element to tell the story of a motion picture or a television program has been known since the dawn of motion pictures communication as the *"Principle of Visual Primacy."* Learning from its forerunner, television makers acknowledged the significance of the picture element in television communication. Some of the do's and don't's for a television commercial in the early days of television urged the writer:

"Don't write a radio commercial for use on television."
"Do show the product and use action in so doing."
"Don't waste words telling what can better be demonstrated."

27

"Don't fail to take advantage of motion, demonstration, and action."
"Do plan the visual portion of the TV commercial first and build
around."(1)

In more recent work on scriptwriting for motion pictures and television,
reliance on the visuals first and on the sound track second is reinforced.
Charles Curran indicated that the writer for the screen must be a good
story-teller who can present his story in terms of images rather than words.
He believed that pantomime expression as a means of communication is at its
highest in television and motion pictures. Accordingly, dialogue should be
kept to a minimum. In his words, "A sheepish smile, a shrug of the
shoulders, or a wink of an eye can carry more impact on the screen than a
paragraph of dialogue."(2)

Television shooting script is a written description of a continuous flow
of visual images supported by sound. An action in a television program is
conceived as a series of shots taken from different points of view. Each point
conveys its own separate "picture statement." Each statement is structured to
move the story of the program. Andreas Feininger explained the need to
recognize individual picture statements that successively portray an idea. He
said, "In comparison to the eye, the lens sees too much - rather than trying to
say everything in one picture, subdivide complex subjects and set-ups and
show them in the form of a short series in which each picture clearly
illustrates only a single point." (3) Usually, a whole television program is
structured from a series of picture statements supported by sound.

## THE VISUAL ELEMENT AND REALITY

In the early days of moving images, the emphasis was put on duplicating
the real thing. The public, marveling at the new invention, enjoyed watching
favorite objects moving on the screen. People were greatly thrilled by the
sight of a train entering a station, or workers leaving a factory at lunch hour.

The success of early films was established through the ability of
filmmakers to present topical and scenic films to the early audience of motion
pictures.

For a period of 25 years from the birth of motion pictures, production of
films flourished on the assumption that the camera visually duplicates what
is put before it. Novices, then, adopted the theater techniques. The action
unfolded in front of the camera. The camera acted as a spectator sitting in the
front row.

As the process of communication through motion pictures evolved,
filmmakers came to realize that the real strength of motion pictures is not in
duplicating reality, but rather in the ability of the camera to manipulate reality
to present the most expressive image of an idea, a concept, a feeling, or a
skill. With this realization, the film art was born, as Arnheim reported. "A

film art developed only gradually when the movie makers began consciously or unconsciously to cultivate the peculiar possibilities of cinematographic techniques and to apply them toward the creation of artistic production." (4)

A few factors led to this stage of development. Among them were luck, chance and the need to physically move the camera closer to the action to record details, such as a nervous twitch, or a wink of an eye reflecting the inner emotions of the actors. It became clear that the power of motion pictures is not its ability to reproduce an action, but rather in its ability to intensify, abridge and reorganize the real world, focusing the attention of an audience on significant details, moving the spectator through an arranged and selected sequence of visual cues. (5) The whole visible world became at the command of the movie maker. In the words of Spottiswoode:

> There is no object too large or so small that he (the film director) cannot compass it with his camera; he may withdraw it until the vastest objects come within its field, or advance it until, with the aid of the microscope, he has sufficiently enlarged the most minute. He need not restrict the sections of the world to their natural places; but may reduplicate them on his strip of film or juxtapose them even though in nature they were far apart. His record of things as they are, or of multiple movements and composite shots, may be projected on the whole screen, or reduced until the significant part occupies only one-thousandth of its area. (6)

Appreciating the difference between reality seen and reality televised, the TV maker selects what will visually better express his purpose of the shot. In making his selection, decisions have to be made on several items, such as: how to compose the shot, what items in the scene the camera will emphasize, the angle of view of the camera, the position of the camera in relation to the scene, and the duration of the shot. Practicing this selection, moving-images recording is not a simple rcording of an event taking place in front of the lens, but a peculiar form of representation of that event. Pudovkin expressed this idea saying:

> Between the natural event and its appearance upon the screen there is a marked difference. It is exactly *this difference that makes the film an art.* Guided by the director, the camera assumes the task of removing every superfluity and directing the attention of the spectator in such a way that he shall see only that which is significant and characteristic. (7)

This practice is not only true in the treatment of dramatic topics. It is also true with factual subjects. A moving image representation of a simple object is never absolutely identical to the real object. A television image of a simple object is an electronic-optical interpretation of that object which modifies some of its characteristics. Nilsen expressed the concept of 'optical interpretations' saying:

> We use the term "interpretation" deliberately, for the cinematic representation is never absolutely identical with the reality subjected to transmission. In all cases it is a specific optical treatment of the object, more or less modifying its character and even its content significance. Even those films we are accustomed to call "documentary" really give us a greater or lesser degree of approximation to simple transmission of the true geometrical relationships and physical qualities of the object photographed. A photograph is by no means a complete and whole reflection of reality. (8)

This very difference between reality seen and reality filmed institutes the cinema's, and eventually the television's peculiar ways of expression. It is the source of much of the enjoyment as well as influence television has on its audience. Accordingly, understanding that difference is absolutely necessary to becoming a critical viewer of television.

## EXTENDING HUMAN VISION

The motion picture and television camera can practically reproduce and optically interpret anything that can be seen. Moreover, the camera extends our vision. Mounting the camera on a microscope, magnified moving images of living microorganisms can be produced. Mounting the camera on a telescope, distant objects can be brought closer to the viewer. Sending a camera on a spacecraft, close-up images of far-away planets are made available for detailed study.

While the television camera can reproduce anything that can be seen, animation can reproduce anything that can be imagined. Animation knows no boundaries. It can visualize the invisible and solidify the intangible. It can re-create physical objects that are extinct, and it can re-create events that happened in the past, or could happen in the future.

Animation can give life to things, go beyond reality, simplify things and actions, add humor to facts, visualize abstractions and allow for free play of the imagination.

Integrating animation with live action in the scene extends the potentiality of the medium by compounding its ability to incorporate the art of animation with live action. Moreover, composite video images produced through the application of chromakey effects, multiple editing, optical, mechanical and electronic effects can enhance a communication situation in which integrated visuals within one shot present stories and events in a unique and a different way.

## THE IMPLYING IMAGE

The visual element in television can do more than represent and interpret reality, extend our human vision, or compose an expressive montage of images. Through the power of symbolism, pictures can imply meanings and feelings. Often, television programs and television spots use images to imply claims or statements without explicitly stating them. As early as 1949, a one-minute commercial, *Father Time and the Motor Block,* employed identifiable visual symbols. Animated "Father Time" symbolized the aging car. The family "cat" symbolized the nine lives of the car. "Scottie," the "repair dog," symbolized thriftiness and loyalty of Chevrolet mechanics. The happy ending was depicted in a scene showing "Father Time" and the family cat riding gleefully in the back seat of the car. The narration accompanying that scene underlined that happy ending: "Now the old car starts quick as a cat, purrs along like a kitten, and the owner no longer feeds the kitty to pay for repairs and upkeep." The last scene of the commercial showed the Chevrolet Service logo, with the family cat behind, delivering the last punchline, "For your car, old age needn't be a cat-astrophe!" (1,p.198-201)

Using the visual element to symbolize personalities, ideas, emotional state, etc. to which the viewer can relate is a very effective persuasive technique in television communication. Television producers have found that the power to visually imply a meaning or a feeling through symbolic images is particularly strong due to the fact that the implied meaning is instantaneously understood. The image of what appears to be a restless person, nervously pacing the room, and occasionally looking in the direction of a telephone in the foreground instantly implies his state of anxiety and his nervous expectation of a telephone call.

The scene of a man sitting at a table smoking a cigarette, and in front of him an ashtray filled with enormous cigarette ends, some of them crushed, and some still lit, implies the length of time the man has spent, and his state of excitement.

Moreover, an image of a slender person holding a diet drink implies the "no calorie" fact, and a smile on her face as she drinks implies the good taste.

Implied messages are communicated to the viewers without activating their perceptual defense mechanism. Accordingly, the possibility of the viewer's acceptance of the message is increased. In this sense, the implied message has a similar power and effect of subliminal messages.

Faced with the challenge of capturing the attention of a noncaptive audience and selling a product in less than 30 seconds, advertisers efficiently use the "implying" characteristic of the visual element in television commercials. In an analysis of television commercials on dairy products (9),

31

it was found that images were designed to tell something not mentioned in the soundtrack. For instance, the packaging of some products such as ice cream invariably showed condensation on the outside to emphasize freshness. The scooping motion of the product was sometimes done in slow motion to emphasize the smoothness of the ice cream. The mouth, tongue and lips played an exaggerated role in the eating of the product to emphasize the taste.

The implying image in commercials is used to portray more than characteristics of the product. (10) Often it is used to make social statements. For instance, in a spot sponsored by the League of Women Voters "Vote (1972)," the verbal message, "On November 7, go out and help someone vote," was repeated three times during the 60-second commercial. Six different situations showing people representing different sectors of the society were presented. (11) The images of these situations implied more than just presenting a cross-section of the American people. They implied statements on social interaction between sectors of the public. Those situations were:

1. An old white woman replacing a black construction worker in operating a jackhammer in the street.
2. A black girl replacing a white policeman in directing traffic.
3. A white cleaning woman replacing the chairman of a board meeting of seven white men.
4. A white man replacing a black dentist who was treating a white man.
5. A white man replacing a white female dancer in a group of six female white and black dancers.
6. A hippie taking the place of the wife of an old farmer as apparently the man and the wife were posing for a picture to be taken.

Too often, the images imply a style of life. The product is associated with a gleeful and glamorous way of living. With the emerging fad of designer jeans, this approach was often used to imply a life-style associated with people wearing designer jeans.

In a Jordache jean commercial, the opening was a scene of a young adult male walking through the hall of an office building where he apparently worked. His attire was business-like. As he passed people in the corridor, they turned their heads to eye him in admiration.

The second scene showed the outside of the office building as the male character was leaving to a sports car shown parked in front of the building. As he got into his convertible and drove off, a close-up shot of the license plate read "JORDACHE" and carried the Jordache insignia. Music and lyrics, "You've got the look," continued throughout the two scenes.

The third scene took us inside a beautifully furnished apartment of the male character. He was shown putting on casual Jordache attire. The lyrics, "You've got the look I want to know better," accompanied this scene and continued into the next scene, "You've got the look that's all together," in which we saw the male character seated in his car, a young adult female exiting from a plush apartment building, and a doorman holding open the car door for her. The female character was seen dressed in a sweater, jacket and white baggy-style Jordache jeans.

The commercial continued to show us the two main characters watching a football game, and dancing in a discotheque as the lyrics continued, "Workin', playin', day or night, Jordache has the fit that's right."

The last scene depicted the two main characters in an outside romantic scene along the coast of New York City. As the camera widens, the shot included the sports car in the forefront of the picture. The lyrics ended, "The Jordache look."

In that commercial, a style of life was visually implied and associated with beautiful, successful and well-to-do young men and women who enjoy working, playing and romantic evenings.

---

To practice one's will to accept or disapprove a message presented through the power of visual implication, a critical viewer of television needs to understand the intricacies of the visual element of television, and to detect the 'unspoken' message in a television presentation.

# REFERENCES

1. Seehafer, E. F. & J.W. Laemmar. *Successful Radio and Television Advertising.* New York: McGraw Hill Book Company, Inc., 5th Edition, 1951, p.197.
2. Curran, Charles. *Screen Writing and Production Techniques.* N.Y.: Hastings House, 1958.
3. Feininger, Andreas. *The Creative Photographer,* Prentice-Hall, 1955, p.20.
4. Arnheim, Rudolf. *Film as Art.* Berkeley & Los Angeles: University of California Press, 1957, p.35.
5. Wagner, Robert W. "The Spectator and the Spectacle," *Audio-Visual Communications Review,* Vol. 3, No. 4, Fall, 1955.
6. Spottiswoode, Raymond. A. *Grammar of the Film,* London: Farber and Farber Ltd., 1935. p.114.
7. Pudovkin, V.I. *Film Techinque and Film Acting.* New York: Grove Press, Inc., 1976. p. 86.
8. Nilsen, Vladimir. *The Cinema as a Graphic Art,* Great Britian: Newness Limited p.16.
9. Hefzallah, Ibrahim and M. Swetz. "A Content Analysis of Dairy Products Commercials," Unpublished Report. Fairfield University, CT.
10. Hefzallah, Ibrahim and Paul Maloney. "Content Analysis of TV Commercials," *International Journal of Instructional Media,* Vol. 5(1). 1977-1978.
11. Hefzallah, Ibrahim and Paul Maloney. "Content Analysis of TV Commercials." Moonograph, Fairfield University Library, Fairfield, CT 1975.

# Chapter V

## SOUND IN TELEVISION

*The second element of the basic unit of the television language is sound. Although television is primarily a visual medium, sound plays a significant role in television communications.*

*During the silent era, movies depended entirely on visual expressiveness. The spoken word was replaced by pantomime, and when words were a necessity, titles were used. Much of the art of the silent film lay in the invention of means to overcome the film's limitations due to the absence of sound. Those limitations were removed with the introduction of sound in films.*

*In its first days, the mere presence of sound in movies was an attractive feature, and the art of visual expressiveness in movies suffered. Within the first decade of sound films, the industry reached a comprehensive understanding of sound in film communication; and when television was introduced, the role of sound in film, and subsequently in television, was well established. That role was further enhanced through creative use of sound in television and motion pictures.*

*Understanding the potential role of sound in television is imperative to becoming a critical viewer of television.*

Television is primarily a visual medium in which sound plays a significant role in communicating the program's message. (1)

Television has learned a great deal from the application of sound in motion pictures. A study of the evolution of sound in motion pictures communication will help explain the present use of sound in television.

## HISTORICAL REVIEW OF SOUND IN MOTION PICTURES COMMUNICATION

During the silent film era, movies depended entirely on visual expressiveness. The spoken word was replaced by pantomime, and when words were a necessity, titles were used. The absence of the spoken words helped to concentrate the spectators' attention more closely on the visible aspect of behavior, and accordingly, the whole event drew particular interest to itself. (2)

35

Giving an example of Chaplin's technique, Rudolph Arnheim claimed that by merely robbing the real event of sound, the appeal of the episode is heightened. For instance:

> He (Chaplin) does not say he is pleased that some pretty girls are coming to see him, but performs the silent dance, in which two bread rolls stuck on a fork act as dancing feet on the table *(The Gold Rush)*. He does not argue, he fights. He avows his love by smiling, swaying his shoulders, and moving his hat . . . . When he is sorry for a poor girl, he stuffs money into her handbag. (2,pp.106-107)

Faced with the problem of the absence of sound when it was specially needed, filmmakers attempted to visually interpret the sound. For instance, in the film, *The Docks of New York,* a revolver shot is interpreted by the rising of a flock of birds. Arnheim believed that

> Such an effect is not just a contrivance on the part of a director to deal with the evil of silence by using an indirect visual method of explaining to the audience that there has been a bang. On the contrary, a positive artistic effect results from the paraphrase . . . the spectator does not simply infer that a shot has been fired, but he actually *sees* something of the quality of the noise — the suddenness, the abruptness of the rising birds, give visually the exact quality that the shot posses accoustically. (2,pp.107-108)

The same technique was followed to illustrate the presence and effect of music. In Feyder's film *Les Nouveaux Messieurs,* Arnheim reports:

> . . . a political meeting becomes very uproarious, and in order to calm the rising emotions Suzanne puts a coin into a mechanical piano. Immediately the hall is lit up by hundreds of electric bulbs, and now the music chimes in with the agitative speech. The music is not heard: it is a silent film. But Feyder shows the audience excitedly listening to the speaker; and suddenly the faces soften and relax: all the heads begin quite gently to sway in time to the music. The rhythm grows more pronounced until at last the spirit of the dance has seized them all; and they swing their bodies gaily from side to side as if to an unheard word of command. The speaker has to give way to the music . . . by this indirect method. . . . the important part of this music — its rhythm, its power to unite and 'move' men — is conspicuously brought out. (2,p.108)

In the span of three decades, the silent film, depending on pictorial expressiveness, developed into a subtle and highly expressive art form. Much of the art of the silent era lay in the invention of means to circumvent the silent film's limitations due to the absence of natural sound. (3) These limitations were suddenly removed with the introduction of sound in films and "the sounds of the real world had become as much a part of the film as its sights." (3,p.148)

In its first days, the mere presence of sound in movies was an attractive feature. Arthur Knight reported that, "The public's enthusiasm for sound was so strong that attendance leaped from 60,000,000 paid admissions per week in 1927 to 110,000,000 in 1929. When the stock market crashed in the fall of 1929, the impetus provided by the introduction of sound proved strong enough to carry the industry safely through the first years of the depression. By 1930, the silent film was a thing of the past . . ." (3,p.146)

Although sound was a key element in carrying the film industry safely during the depression, artistic communication through movies suffered a set-back. The emphasis shifted from communicating through the moving image to faithfully reproducing sound. The camera was imprisoned inside a sound-proof booth to avoid picking up its noise by the microphones. Action was greatly influenced by the positioning of microphones on the set. The sound man became the king of the motion picture studio. Manvell described the immature use of sound in sound films, then, as follows:

> Whole plays were transferred to the screen with the camera following the dialogue around the set like a lap-dog terrified of being left alone. It was a depressing return to adolescence and cheap effect. The equipment was expensive, and by God it must be used, and used it was, until the directors and the public wearied of it, and decided that, after all, you went to see and not merely to hear a film. (4)

In time, the advantages and limitations of this technical gift — the sound — were realized. It was recognized that by introducing sound "the break-up of the illusion caused by the titles flashed on the screen for as long as it took the slowest reader to spell them out could now be forgotten. *The film could speak for itself."* (4)

In 1933, Arnheim noted the role of sound in talking pictures:

> Sound film — at any rate real sound film — is not a verbal masterpiece supplemented by pictures, but a homogeneous creation of word and picture which cannot be split up into parts that have any meaning separately. (4,p.53)

By 1941 with the production of *Citizen Kane,* the industry had reached a comprehensive understanding of sound and pictures in motion picture communication. When television joined the mass media family, the theory of sound and images in motion picture and television communication was well established. Emphasis was put upon integrating pictures and sound. In answering the question, "How does one use sound?" Cushman (1957) said, ". . . by making it so much a part of the picture that it isn't a picture at all without it." (5) In his words, "Sound properly used can aid in establishing a scene or in setting a locale. It can establish or accent a mood. It can strengthen continuity, heighten a dramatic point and generally speed up action." (5) Sound in motion pictures, according to Hoban, not only adds to an increased sense of realism, it also helps interpret the picture. (6) However, according to the principle of visual primacy, the movie maker should strive to make the pictures tell the story, as White (1956) said ". . . the spoken word, the sound effects, and the music should *reinforce a pictorial communication* that can stand alone." (7) Recently, a more dynamic relationship between sound and picture elements has been expressed by Walter Murch (1981). In his view, sound and pictures in motion pictures are like partners in a dance. In an interview with Frank Paine, Walter Murch explained this idea as follows:

> Image and sound are linked together in a dance. And like some kinds of dance, they do not always have to be clasping each other around the waist: they can go off and dance on their own, in a kind of ballet. There are times when they must touch, there must be moments when they make some sort of contact, but then they can be off again. There are some films where the contact is unbroken: the image leads and the sound follows — it never deviates from what you actually see, what is directly indicated. Other films are way out there — what you are hearing has only the smallest physical relationship to the image. Yet there is — there has to be — some kind of connection being made, a mental connection. Out of the juxtaposition of what the sound is telling you and what the picture is telling you, you (the audience) come up with a third idea which is composed of *both* picture and sound and resolves their superficial differences. The more dissimilar you can get between picture and sound, and yet still retain a link of some sort, the more powerful the effect. (8)

## HOW SOUND IS USED IN
## TELEVISION COMMUNICATION

Sound in television is used in a variety of ways to achieve more viewers' involvement in the program. Understanding the techniques of using sound in television is imperative to becoming a critical viewer. The uses of sound in television can be one or more of the following:

1. *Realistic Sound:* Natural sounds are often used to add a sense of reality to the portrayed scene. Viewers do not only see what things look like, but can hear how they sound. The reproduced sound travels

through the air to reach our ears and to vibrate our bodies. It envelops us in a fashion similar to our actual presence in the scene. Magnifying the loudness of the recorded sound can have even greater impact as our bodies vibrate more vigorously. "Soundrama" movies such as *Midway* engulf the spectator with sound waves in an attempt to duplicate reality and maximize the spectators' involvement in the scene. Stereo television broadcast can enhance the viewers' involvement as more sound cues are received.

2. ***Relevant Sound:*** Out of the many audio messages in reality, the television maker selects only those that are relevant to the scene and removes any irrelevant sounds that might distract the viewer's attention. Isolating relevant sounds emphasizes their importance and maximizes their impact. The spectator is not only compelled to hear those sounds but he also approaches the situation with unspoken realization that selected sounds must be important, otherwise, the director would have deleted them.

3. ***Exaggerated Sound:*** Sometimes selected sounds in a scene are not faithfully reproduced in terms of their relative natural intensity or frequency. Distortion of some sounds and relative magnification of certain sounds are used to compose an expressive sound track that will communicate the mood of the scene. For example, the muffled voice of the captain in charge of hanging the prisoner in *Occurrence at Owl Creek Bridge* established a mood of the scene as the director led us into a mental journey of the prisoner's attempts to escape his fate.

In explaining how the interpretation of a scene is affected by the selection and blending of a set of sounds, Millerson gave the following example:

> Imagine, ... the slow, even, toll of a cathedral bell, accompanied by the rapid footsteps of approaching churchgoers. We could reproduce these sounds simply as they happen to arise, or we could deliberately draw attention to particular aspects, in order to give the sounds a certain significance:
>> The quiet, insignificant bell, ... against the loud footsteps.
>> The bell's slow dignity, contrasted with restless footsteps.
>> The bell's lingering echoes, contrasted with the staccato impatience of footsteps.
>> Its boom, overwhelming all other sounds. (9)

Selective presentation of sound helps set location, suggests a mood, builds up expectations, and emotionally involves the viewer in the portrayed action.

4. **Silence:** A television program does not usually use sound in every scene. Silence, the absence of sound, is often used very effectively. Silent moments in a sound program permit the viewer to respond internally to the scene, and thus increase viewers' involvement.

5. **Post-Synchronization of Sound:** Sound is not usually recorded at the time the picture is recorded. In many instances, sound is added to the picture in the post-production phase of the program. Post-synchronization of sound allows the producer to compose a creative sound track from human voices, sound effects, and music. Since the producer is not confined to the time and space of recording the picture, post-synchronization gives him/her the opportunity to manipulate different audio inputs in creating an expressive sound track.

6. **Asynchronous Sound:** Sound reproduced does not have to match the picture on the screen. For instance, one could hear the sound of a closing door without actually seeing the door being closed. Or, in a conversation scene, we hear the voice of one actor while we see the picture of the second actor. Such an approach allows the viewer to see the reaction of a person to the sound.

7. **Contrasting Sound:** Sound sometimes is played against, rather than with, the images. Adding a new dimension to the scene, a new meaning emerges. For example, in *The Victors,* a deserter was about to be shot by a squad from his own company. The ground was covered with snow. It was Christmas time. Accompanying the picture of the squad marching to where their fellow soldier was to be executed was Christmas carols. One could not help going beyond the knowledge that the deserter was to be executed, to reflect on war, man against his brother, and peace symbolized by Christmas.

8. **Sound as a Transition Technique:** Sometimes sound is used as a transition between scenes. In many programs, the sound track of a new scene is heard in the background of the preceding scene prior to cutting to the new scene. For example, in *The Defiants,* a group of people were in pursuit of two prisoners who had escaped from a prison truck. A member of the pursuing group had a portable radio on. Prior to cutting from the escaping prisoners to the pursuing group, the sound of the radio is heard. Perceived rather on a subliminal level, the viewer expected abrupt change of the scene.

9. **Symbolic Sound:** Symbolic sound can sometimes interpret the action more than the use of realistic synchronized sound. For instance, in *Citizen Kane,* in an argument scene between Mr. Kane and his second wife, Mr. Kane slapped his wife. Mrs. Kane did not utter a sound

reflecting her personal agony. Instead, a sound of a girl crying in pain was heard in the background. Another example comes from a film about a bank robbery in which the robbers escape on a train. The scheming man was getting rid of his accomplices one by one. In a murder scene of one of his accomplices, the director cuts from the movements of the killer's hand stabbing the victim to the exterior of the train showing the train rushing at a high speed. The direction of the train in the scene was the same as that of the hand symbolizing the aggressive, cold act of killing. The high-pitched train whistle symbolized the agony of the victim.

10. *Abstract Sound:* Sound could be synthetic. The first synthetic sound track was used by Mamoulian in the production of the early version of *Dr. Jekyll and Mr. Hyde* (1932). The sound track was built "from exaggerated heartbeats mingled with the reverberations of gongs played backwards, bells heard through echo chambers, and completely artificial sounds created by photographing light frequencies directly onto the sound track."(3,p.165). The effects were post-synchronized with the transformation of Dr. Jekyll to Mr. Hyde.

Artificial or abstract sound, if consistently synchronized with an abstract or unfamiliar visual, will be accepted as the visual's natural sound, for example, the ascending whine of the transporter in *Star Trek*.

11. *Subjective Sound:* Realistic, exaggerated, or symbolic sounds presented from the performer's subjective view can reveal what goes on in his/her mind. Sound flash-back, for instance, can show the performer's reaction to a situation based on his/her past experiences. Key sounds or words repeated could reveal the inner tension a performer is experiencing. For instance, in Alfred Hitchcock's *Blackmail,* in self-defense, a girl murdered an artist in his studio with a bread-knife. In the breakfast scene, the word "knife" was repeated to expose the girl's state of tension, as Ernest Lindgren reported:

> All night she walks through the street in a daze, creeping home to bed in the early morning just before her mother comes to call her. At breakfast she is nervous, distraught, her experiences of the previous night, and the lack of sleep, have left her in a state bordering on hysteria. A gossiping woman neighbor comes in to talk to the girl's parents. She is full of the details of the murder spread across the morning newspapers. In her harsh metallic voice she speaks of the knife which has been found. Again she mentions the word 'knife.' The girl is asked by her father to cut some bread: a close shot shows the look of

terror staring from her eyes. The woman's gossip has become a continuous mumble in which only one word is heard clearly at intervals: 'knife - knife - knife.' The girl stretches out her hand for the bread-knife, and as she touches it, the word 'knife' is suddenly shouted out, and she drops it with a clatter; in the silence which follows, everyone stares at her in amazement. (10)

Understanding how sound is used in moving-images communication is imperative to the development of one's critical viewing abilities, as one becomes aware of the persuasive intentions of the telecast.

## THE ELEMENTS OF SOUND

Sound is composed from three elements: spoken language, sound effects, and music. These three elements are selected and integrated to form the sound track of the program.

The integration of these three elements is not just a mere addition. It is more or less like a chemical compound in which elements forming that compound are fused together. The result is a powerful element of communication that is more effective than its components.

The choice of those components is made either to capture a realistic representation of the natural sound of an event, or to produce an artistically expressive representation of an event, as we have previously discussed. The director has to decide which sound components are relevant to the structure of the sound track, and how those components can be manifested to compose the most expressive sound track. Imperative to making this decision is his/her understanding of the role of each of the sound components in television communication. The following is a brief discussion of these three basic components.

### *Spoken Language*

The verbal content of the sound track, whether a monologue or a dialogue, should be easily understood. The comprehension time of the screen is limited; thus, words are selected to convey the intended meaning upon hearing. As early as the days of silent movies, simple and direct verbal communication was advocated in silent movie titles. In the words of Pudovkin:

Superfluous words that may enhance the literary beauty of the sentence but will complicate the rapid comprehension are not permissible. The film spectator has no time to savour words. The title must get to the spectator quickly. (11)

42

Usually, the television producer looks for simple and easy-to-grasp narration or dialogue. Three factors are considered in judging the suitability of a verbal track: vocabulary level, sentence length, and rate of delivery.(12,13) The vocabulary level of most entertaining programs is below the 4th grade level. Sentences in general tend to be short, and the pace of delivery is not too fast to avoid losing the viewer, nor too slow to avoid boring him/her. Voice intonation, volume, speed, and other paralinguistic elements are intricacies of the spoken components of the sound track. Rules for effective speech delivery and narration are considered carefully to communicate the mood of the scenes and to keep the audience tuned in.

### Sound Effects

Sound effects add realism and accent the scene's moods. Sometimes "a sound effect can become a key signal, carrying with it the principal sense of the scene."(13,p.202) In addition, sound effects can be abstract sounds which accompany abstract images as Jones indicated:

> Here are two abstract shapes. And here are two abstract words, 'tackety' and 'goloomb.' The words become sounds when spoken, but they have no specific meanings. Yet it is simple to match the abstract words and sounds to the abstract shapes. The angular shape is obviously 'tackety' and the curved one 'goloomb'.(14)

Repeating abstract sounds with abstract images or unfamiliar images can result in accepting the abstract sound as the natural sound of abstract images.

Data available on the function of sound effects in moving-images communication are meager, but it seems reasonable to assume that the intelligent use of "sound effects" can help communicate better the program's message. (15) This is especially true with the use of high fidelity sound recording and playback systems through which well-reproduced sound can engulf the viewer and maximize the viewers' involvement in the scene.

### Music

In discussing the place of music in film, Kendall indicated the ability of music to communicate non-verbal meanings. He said:

> Music is a symbolic form. It articulates concepts frequently difficult to express in language or in photographs. It symbolizes moods and

feelings, emotions and tensions. The fact that we cannot always name the mood, emotion, or tension conveyed by *music is in itself evidence* of the symbolic character of music, and its ability *to communicate meanings which are not verbal.* (16)

In reviewing literature on music in motion pictures, Zuckerman (1949) indicated three functions: informational, emotional, and conceptual and integrative. The informational functions of music were considered as: (a) the delineation of a personality or a character, (b) provision of subjective evaluation for an objective image, (c) putting emphasis on action, (d) telling a story, (e) recalling past events, and (f) foretelling the future. The emotional functions of music were indicated as: (a) establishing atmosphere or mood, (b) adding to the emotional tone or mode of the incident, and (c) pointing up dramatic or comic highlights of the scene. The conceptual and integrative functions were believed to be: (a) unification of dramatic material, (b) association of ideas, (c) connection of dialogue sequences, and (d) accompaniment for sequences of silent action. (17)

Charles Berg (1979) indicated five basic functions of music in film and television:

(a) To mask noise and neutralize disagreeable sounds emanating from sources within and outside of the viewing environment;

(b) To avoid silence and fill the disturbing aural voids when other audio stimuli are absent;

(c) To provide continuity and undergird the program's sequencing of separate images with a cohesive bond;

(d) To provide dramatic support that amplifies and reinforces the program's effect on the audience;

(e) To use music as a special feature to attract viewers. (18)

In a recent study on the effect of background music on film understanding and emotional responses of American Indians, Josephine Raburn and LaWanda Tyson (1980) indicated that sound, even when it was only background music with minimal sound effects seemed to be essential to the understanding of film. (19)

Newlin Dika (1977) talked of music as a major component of film that has been so since the "silent era." He indicated that "There was an early recognition that film, in itself a 'cold' medium, needed the warmth that music alone can provide." In his opinion, music can accomplish the following tasks:

1. It can set mood.

2. It can reinforce an action by mimicking its rhythms exactly. (This

44

technique is common in animated cartoons.)

3. It can serve to contrast with the visual element on the screen. (For example, in *Spellbound* the weird wailing electric sound of the theremin indicated the sinister meaning hidden behind homely unterrifying sights such as a glass of milk, and an all-white bathroom.)

4. It can set the locale.

5. It can suggest a principal ethnic group in the story such as use of drum-beats and heavy rhythmic chanting for American Indians.

6. It can set the period of the film (often done through the authentic music and instruments of the film's period).

7. It can correct errors made by others in the production team. (The composer's correct choice of tempo can compensate for actions that might appear too fast or too slow.) (20)

To summarize, music is an intricate component of the television sound track. Its role goes beyond setting the mood, the locale, and the time of the scene as it interacts with the visual element of the program, as well as the other audio elements reinforcing action and suggesting new meanings and feelings.

———————

Intelligent selection of sound components and the ways that they are recorded in relation to each other and in relation to the synchronized images can maximize the impact of a television program as each component of the sound track interacts with the image to capture the attention of the viewer. A critical viewer of television needs to be aware of the dynamic interaction between sound elements and the visual element which produces a captivating television experience.

# REFERENCES

1   Hefzallah, Ibrahim. "Visual Primacy, Reality, and the Implying Image in Motion Pictures and TV," *International Journal of Instructional Media,* Volume 12, No. 3, 1985. pp.157-166.

2.  Arnheim, Rudolf. *Film as Art.* Berkeley & Los Angeles: University of California Press, 1957. p.110.

3.  Knight, Arthur. *The Liveliest Art, A Panoramic History of the Movies,* A Mentor Book, 1979. p.148.

4.  Manvell, Roger. *Film.* London: Pelican Books, 1944. p.53.

5.  Cushman, George W. "Use Sound with a Purpose," *American Cinematographer,* Sept. 1957. pp.588-97.

6.  Hoban, Charles, Jr. *Focus on Learning.* Washington D.C.: American Council on Education, 1952. p.27.

7.  White, Ralph "Planning Films that Teach." *Audio Visual Communication Review,* Spring, 1956.

8.  Paine, Frank "Sound Design." *Journal of the University Film Association,* XXXIII, 4 (Fall 1981). p.15.

9.  Millerson, Gerald. *The Technique of Television Production,* 9th Revised Edition, New York: Hastings House, 1974. p.327.

10. Lindgren, Ernest. *The Art of the Film,* London: George Allen & Unwin Ltd., 1955. pp.108-109.

11. Pudvokin, V.I. *Film Technique and Film Acting.* New York: Grove Press, Inc., 1976. p.61.

12. Park, J.J. "Vocabulary & Comprehension Difficulties of Sound Motion Pictures," *School Review,* 53:154-161, March 1945.

13. Wagner, Robert W. "Design in the Education Film: An Analysis of Production Elements in Twenty-One Widely Used Non-Theatrical Motion Pictures," unpublished Ph.D. dissertation, Ohio State University, 1953, p.90.

14. Jones, C. "Music and the Animated Cartoon," *Hollywood Quarterly,* 1:364-370, July 1946.

15. Neu, D.M. "The Effect of Attention-Gaining Devices on Film-Mediated Learning," unpublished Ph.D. dissertation, Penn. State University, 1950, p.76.

16. Kendall, K. "Film Production Principles — The Subject of Research," *Journal of Soc. Mot. Pict. and Eng.,* 58:428, May, 1952.

17. Zuckerman, John V. *Music in Motion Pictures — Review of Literature with Implications for Instructional Films,* Office of Naval Research, Port Washington, N.Y., Special Devices Center, 1949.

18. Berg, Charles M. "Correcting the Visual Bias: Assessing the Functions of Music in Film and Television," ERIC, ED113772.

19. Raburn, Josephine & LaWanda, Tyson. "Test Score Results by Sex and Perceptual Type When Background Music Accompanies Film, Filmstrip, and Lecture Presentations," ERIC, ED196412.

20. Dika, Newlin. "Music for the Flickering Image: American Film Scores," *Music Education Journal.* 64;1; 24-35, Sept. 1977.

# Chapter VI
## THE SYNTAX
## OF TELEVISION

*It is imperative to becoming a critical viewer to understand how shots are composed, sequenced, and edited to depict meanings and feelings with the intention of involving the viewer in the program.*

*In television, shots that have a pictorial unity are joined to form a sequence. A sequence is an episodic portion of the television program characterized by an inherent unity. Sequences are joined together to form the program.*

*Shots and sequences may be joined together simply by cutting from one to the other, or by employing a variety of techniques known as special effects. Cuts and special effects can be viewed as the punctuation of the discursive language of television which editors have to use to compose a continuous program. Since editors have different styles in editing a program, we can look at editing as the style of the television language.*

*Therefore, to study the syntax and the style of the television language, it is necessary to study: (a) its basic units: the shots, (b) its punctuation or transition techniques, and (c) its style: editing.*

## THE BASIC UNIT OF THE TELEVISION LANGUAGE: THE SHOT

### Active vs. Passive Shots

The shot in television is similar to the word in the verbal language in terms of being the building block from which expression is structured. In the early days of motion pictures, a continuous shooting of an event was considered to be the way through which the moviemaker could present a meaningful visual experience to the audience. The camera replaced the audience and acted as a spectator in the first row.

To encompass all the action without losing any parts, the camera was usually set at a distance to ensure a wide view. It was considered ill-practice of the cameraman to show only a part of the actor's body. The margins of the screen were not supposed to cut parts of anything.

In those days the camera was a passive spectator. In time this function changed and the camera became an active observer. In the words of Pudvokin:

> The Americans were the first to seek to replace an active observer ... by means of the *camera*. They showed in their work that it was not only possible to record the scene shot, but that by maneuvering with the camera itself in such a way that its position in relation to the object shot varied several times — it was made possible to reproduce the same scene in far clearer and more expressive form than with the lens playing the part of a theatre spectator sitting fast in his stall. The camera, at last, received a change of *life*. It acquired the faculty of movement on its own, and transformed itself from a *spectator* to an active *observer*. Henceforward, the camera, controlled by the director, could not merely enable the spectator to see the object shot, but could introduce him to apprehend it.
>
> It was at this moment that the concepts *close-up, mid-shot*, and *long-shot* first appeared in cinematography. (1,pp.82-83)

## The Three-Basic-Shots Formula

David Wark Griffith is credited with being the first person to fully exploit the use of the close-up and the extreme-close-up shots, and to standardize a basic shot plan which involved the long shot, the medium shot, and the close-up shots.

Griffith used his first close-up shot in the film *For Love of Gold*. Faced with the problem of making the audience aware of a growing distrust between two thieves, he moved the camera closer for a large full-length view of the actors to reveal their facial expressions.

Later, in his film *After Many Years,* 1908, he moved his camera closer to the actor than he did in *For Love of Gold,* and the close-up shot became the dramatic complement of the long shots. (2,p.282)

Despite all the advances in motion pictures and television camera techniques, the basic formula in televising an action is as follows:

a. a long shot, or an orientation shot to introduce the subject within his/her locale to the audience;

b. a medium shot which narrows the attention of the audience to the subject and pertinent sections of the background;

c. a close-up shot which isolates the subject from the background and provides the audience with detailed information.

The three-basic shots formula: long, medium, and close-up, resembles our practice of subjective perception in almost every daily life activity. For instance, let us assume that you are going shopping in a store you have never been to before. As you get into the store, you first scan the store to orient yourself with the general ambience of the store and to establish your bearings. Your view encompasses a wide angle of the store. In television language this is known as a long shot. Its main function is to orient you with your new locale.

Next, you zero-in on one section of the store which probably carries what you are interested in purchasing. In doing that, you exlcuded almost every other section of the store. In television language, this is known as a medium shot. Its main function is to help the viewer to pay closer attention to the segments of the main event being portrayed on the screen.

As you reach your section, your eyes search for the particular item you are looking for, and once you locate it, you concentrate your attention on that item. Everything else in your field of vision becomes relatively insignificant. In television language this is known as a close-up shot. Its main function is to help the viewer to concentrate on specific detail in the field of view.

From the above example, one can see some similarity between how we deal with our visual world in real life and how we present it on the television screen. However, there are differences. In reality we maintain the field of view but our attention shifts from a wide to a narrow vision in which one item occupies our attention, while everything else falls outside our attention margin.

The three shots are the basic shots which the television maker uses to construct a smooth, visually continuous program. Individual shots are juxtaposed using a variety of transition techniques to achieve smooth visual continuity between the various shots. These transition techniques are similar to the punctuation of the verbal language. In the following pages a brief discussion of the most commonly used transition techniques known as optical/electronic effects is presented.

## TRANSITION

### *Optical/Electronic Effects*

Optical/electronic effects are achieved by manipulating the camera's lens and/or the special effects generator or switcher. These effects are: cut, fade-in and fade-out, dissolve, wipe, out-of-focus, refocus, rack focusing, and a host of new digital visual effects. Of all these effects, the cut is the most commonly used transition technique.

51

## *The Cut*

Within one scene, the cut is the method of getting from one camera to another when the action is continuous and when there is no indication of lapse in time. Two possible production techniques are usually used. In the first, a multiple-camera system is used. The director calls the shots which will insure the continuity of the scene. Switching from one camera to the other, the director selects the best angle of view of the action being televised.

In the second technique, a single camera is used. the camera has to be moved or adjusted whenever the director changes the angle of view of the scene being televised. Later, in post-production, the camera shots are juxtaposed one after the other to form a continuous visual flow of the televised action.

The cut is also used to compose a montage of short shots that are conceptually related. For instance, in many news and documentary shows, the technique is used to present the reaction of different people to a question posed to them by an interviewer. Usually the interviewer is shown at the beginning posing the question to an individual. The rest of the sequence will show different people's reactions without repeating the question.

Cuts are also used to join sequences taking place in different locales. They could be either simultaneously happening or a time lapse existed between them. In either case, the sequences will have a bearing on each other. For instance, cuts were used to join the sequences of the pursuers and the escaped prisoners in *The Defiant Ones*. In that film a group of people were in pursuit of two prisoners who escaped from a prison truck. A member of the pursuing group had a portable radio on. Prior to cutting from the escaping prisoners to the pursuing group, the sound of the radio was heard. Perceived rather on a subliminal level, the viewer expected the change of scene. Making the viewer aware of the change in scenery about to happen when using the cut as a transitional technique is called motivating the cut. When properly used, the viewer is moved from one location to another and from one moment of time to another without hindering the viewer's comprehension of the program's continuity.

Sometimes intervening shots are interlaced within a continuum of shots. Two types of cuts are often practiced: cut-ins and cut-aways. (3) Both types are vital to the comprehension of the screen's happenings. The cut-in shot cuts into the main action to bring the audience closer to an intricate point of the action. For instance, two people meet in a medium shot. There is something mysterious or peculiar about their handshake. The director cuts to a close-up shot of the handshake, or to an extreme close-up shot of a ring worn by the actors identifying them as members of a secret group.

The cut-away cuts away from the main action to a related subject to enhance the main line of the story. For instance, in the previous example, if the two people are watched by an undercover agent, the director will cut to a medium-long shot to establish their meeting as being watched by a third person.

## Fade-In and -Out

By fade-in is meant the gradual appearance of the picture on the screen, and by fade-out is meant its gradual disappearance.

Fades are used to keep one scene distinct from the next. Sometimes if scenes follow one another without a break in the visual, they might appear to be a part of an unbroken time sequence. To show that an episode has come to an end, the last scene is faded out, and to show that a new episode is about to start, the first scene of the new episode is faded in. A fade-in, in this sense, is similar to the opening of the curtain in the theatre, and a fade-out is similar to closing the curtain on the last scene in a play.

Use of the fades to end a sequence is especially recommended when the sequence is carried out in a retarded tempo. For instance, a man exhaustedly approaches an armchair, lowers himself into it, drops his head in his hands. After a short pause, the director slowly fades out the picture.

Fades have a rhythmic significance. There are slow fades and quick fades. The choice of the speed depends on the rhythm of the action.

Sometimes for the sake of giving the impression of a change in locale or in time, a fast fade-out is followed with a fast fade-in. This is usually done when the spectator has to keep in mind the first sequence and relate it to the new sequence.

Fading-in and fading-out can be used to show people's subjective perception, (4) if for instance, the actor is waking up or falling asleep. However, fades are commonly used to begin and to end a scene, a sequence, or the program.

## Dissolves

Superimposing a fade-out on a fade-in results in an effect known as a dissolve. On the screen, one image gradually appears through the other. The effect is achieved through the use of a video switcher.

A dissolve is a softer transition than the cut. The dissolve is an excellent technique to show the birth of an idea from another or the visual relationship between two or more objects or subjects. (5) For instance, a series of dissolving pictures of the round sun, into a full moon, into concentric circles created on the surface of water when a pebble is thrown, into a crude circular stone similar to that used by prehistoric man to roll heavy weights, into an image of the wheel of an early cart, and finally into the image of the modern wheel could show the possible origin of the modern wheel from the early conceptualization of roundness to the application of that concept in precivilization time to the present-day application.

Visual relationships could also be presented by a series of dissolves. For instance, the image of a son dissolving into the image of his father to show the resemblance between the two, or an image of Indian folk-art dissolving into an image of Middle-East folk-art to show the similarity between the two arts.

Television commercials use a great deal of dissolves in presenting a variety of rich visuals selling the product where one image is visually related to the other, thus making a tremendous visual statement about the product in the short span of 30-seconds.

A second use of the dissolve is bridging space and time. For instance, the scene might start with a long shot of a meadow. From a distance, one can see a very beautiful flower-bed. A series of dissolving shots can bridge the distance between the first point of view to that of an ultra-close-up shot of a flower in a matter of seconds.

To emphasize the passage of time, it is also possible to dissolve through a series of images of the same object or subject as it changes its appearance with time. For instance, a series of shots taken of a tree can show the passage of a year going from a full summer green foliage to fall, winter, and spring and summer again.

## Wipes

The third type of optical effect is known as wipe. In this effect, one scene replaces another. Different patterns of wipes can be achieved through the video switcher. The simple types of wipes are the horizontal and vertical wipes in which the new image wipes off the old image from the left to the right side of the screen (or vice-versa), or from the bottom to the top (or vice-versa), respectively. Through the miracle of electronics, many facinating and bizarre wipes are used. Usually, wipes attract the attention of the viewer. In some instances, the viewer may be distracted from the main message of the program.

Wipes are usually used to present a succeeding stage of the story. For example, if a man leaves a room and enters another in a completely different locality, a sense of continuous action can be achieved by a wipe moving in the same direction as the action.

Wipes can also be used to present simultaneous action; for instance, two people walking separately to meet each other. The image of the first person moving from left to right on the screen can be wiped by the image of the second person moving from right to left. The last shot shows the two persons moving in opposite directions, until they meet.

## *Out of Focus/Refocus*

Sometimes the director intentionally throws the end of a scene out of focus, and starts the next scene out of focus. Since the screen stays out of focus for the end of the first scene and the beginning of the second scene, the audience knows that a change in locale and/or time is occurring. Accordingly, the audience becomes motivated to reorient itself to the new scene about to come into focus. This transition is sometimes used in flashback when an actor is remembering his/her childhood, for instance. The transition takes the viewer back in time. A similar transition ends the flashback and puts the viewer back in the actor's contemporary time.

Other times the effect is used to reflect the main actor's subjective perception. For instance, an actor regaining consciousness might see his doctor as an out-of-focus image, which comes gradually into focus as he regains complete consciousness.

## *Rack Focusing*

Rack focusing is a transition technique usually used to direct the attention of the viewer from one point in the shot to another point in the same shot. For instance, in a scene of two people, the director might start the shot with the person in the foreground in focus, and as importance shifts from that person to the person in the background, the director gradually throws the image of the foreground person out of focus simultaneously bringing into focus the image of the person in the background, thus shifting the attention of the viewer to the second person.

## *New Special Effects*

Through innovative digital electronics new special effects are often used in which the image-plane shrinks, rotates, and moves in or outside of the frame to be replaced by another image following the same pattern of effects in an opposite manner. The technique draws attention to itself, but is a powerful transitional device which can probably be used to hold the attention of the viewer as the program moves from one segment to another. It can also be used to show the evolution of an idea, the birth of an idea from another, and/or to illustrate the extraordinary, such as images related to space flights and man's invasion into the world of the unknown.

## EDITING
## *The Style of the TV Language*

In the early days of motion pictures, continuity was achieved by shooting in real time without moving the camera from its place. (6) The camera was placed in one position to record an action unfolding in front of it. For instance, in one of the early films of Lumieres Brothers, *Arrival Of A Train At A Station,* the camera was placed on the platform of a railroad station to film the appearance of the train as a black spot on the horizon, and continued filming for approximately two minutes — the length of that film — showing the train pulling into the station and the disembarking and embarking of passengers. In that film, the camera did not move from its place, nor was its angle of view manipulated to show the event from another perspective. The producers of the film were sure that the position of the camera allowed the photographing of the total event without moving the camera.

In another film, also produced in France during the same time period, *Watering the Garden,* the comic action was simple. A gardener was shown watering the garden with a hose. A boy cautiously stepped into the frame and stepped on the hose to prevent the water from flowing. Surprised, the gardener turned the nozzle toward himself, at which time the boy stepped off the hose to restore the flow of the water, drenching the startled gardener. Pursuing the boy to give him a "spank," both the gardener and the boy stepped off the frame. The camera stayed in the same position until the gardener brought the boy with him into the frame of the camera vision, and started spanking him.

In those films there was nothing left to the imagination of the viewer. The structure of the film was a linear structure, one event leading into the other with no lapse of time. To present two events happening simultaneously in *The Great Train Robbery* (1903), Edwin Porter introduced what is known as parallel editing. (7) In parallel editing the audience is shown two events happening simultaneously in two different locales. Each event has a bearing on the other. At the climax point, the two events occur in the same locale. Edwin Porter was the first to introduce this type of story telling in that film in which a group of citizens pursued gangsters who robbed a train. Porter cut from the scene of the pursuers to the gangsters as they attempted to flee. The last scene was the gun fight between the gangsters and the pursuers.

People of that time were thrilled by that movie. It is considered by film historians as a milestone in the development of the art of communication in the motion picture medium. It proved that:

(1)　a central idea can hold segments of film shot in different locations and at different times to tell one story;

(2)　the director can change the position of the camera and still can achieve a sense of continuity on the screen;

56

(3)   the structure of the film is not done in the shooting stage, but in the editing stage;

(4)   bringing two events to converge in one location can add a great deal of excitement in the film as the audience waits in anticipation for the "last-minute rescue."

Further experimentation with film communication through the work of Griffith (6,7) proved that freeing the camera from a fixed position and manipulating it to achieve dramatic effects underlines the art of communication in motion pictures. Griffith also saw that repeatedly interrupting the main event to reveal intricate and unnoticed happenings to the naked eye can enhance dramatic film presentation. To Griffith, a film sequence is made up of incomplete shots whose order and selection are governed by dramatic necessity. From shot to shot the emphasis varies, directing the attention of the viewer to a specific message in the shot, in the scene, and eventually in the total film.

Early Russian filmmakers and theoreticians, analyzing the work of Griffith and experimenting with film persuasion, refined the theory of editing to achieve audience involvement and understanding of a film's message. The main intention of the Russian filmmakers was to indoctrinate the public in the views of the Russian revolution. Regardless of the content, early Russian movies demonstrated an understanding of the syntax of the motion picture language and how it can be used to persuade viewers.

In their writing, both Sergei Eisenstein and Pudvokin indicated that for a film to be kept continually effective, each shot must make a new and specific point. According to Pudvokin:

> In every art there must be firstly a material and secondly a method of composing this material specially adapted to this art. The musician has sound as material and he composes them in time. The painter's materials are color, and he combines them in space on the surface of a canvas . . . the material in filmwork consist of pieces of film. (1,pp.166-167)

Editing became the art of joining shots together, not only to achieve a smooth visual flow of images on the screen, but most importantly, to construct a creative film story. Editing as practiced today in both film and television can be one or all of the following:

(1)   *linear editing* — one act follows the next in the same order in which they happen in real life;

(2)   *parallel editing* — more than one event happening simultaneously, stages of which are presented one after the other. The last shot is usually the climax of the story in which all of the main characters

responsible in all or in part about the parallel events come to one locale to the final statement or ending of the picture. In adventure programs, this moment is usually called the "last-minute rescue;"

(3) ***symbolic editing*** — when images or sound are used to symbolize ideas, feelings, and events. For instance, using a series of dissolves of shots of a tree to show the passage of time as the tree changes in color and in shape with the four seasons; or using the sound of a moving train as a transition from a shot of a landlady discovering the murder of one of her tenants, to the train in which the murderer was escaping;

(4) ***contrast editing*** — images depicting contrasting points of view or conditions follow each other to emphasize the contrast between them, such as shots of a beautiful landscape followed by shots of a polluted landscape; or when sound and images contrast to make an editorial statement; for instance, in *The Victors*, there was a scene of an army deserter who was led to execution by members of his own company. The background was an open landscape covered with snow. The picture of the landscape looked like what one sees on Christmas cards. The sound heard as the soldiers marched to execute their fellow soldier was that of Christmas carols. The meaning derived from this scene goes beyond the literal interpretation of the event to reflect on war as the reason for turning man against his brother.

Active camera shots, expressive punctuation techniques, and the proper style of editing compose the persuading power of television. It is imperative to becoming a critical viewer to understand how shots are composed, sequenced, and edited to depict meanings and feelings with the intention of involving the viewer in the program's happenings.

# REFERENCES

(1) Pudvokin, V.I. *Film Technique & Film Acting,* New York: Groves Press, Inc., 1976.

(2) North, Joseph H., "The Early Development of the Motion Pictures, 1887-1909," unpublished Ph.D. dissertation, Cornell University, 1950. p.282.

(3) Gaskill, Arthur, and Englander, David A., *How To Shoot a Movie Story, The Technique of Pictorial Continuity,* 3rd. Edition, New York: Morgan & Morgan, Inc., 1976.

(4) Arnheim, Rudolf. *Film As Art.* Berkely & Los Angeles: University of California Press, 1957. pp.118-119.

(5) Spottiswoode, Raymond. *A Grammar of the Film,* London: Faber & Faber Limited, 1935. pp.119-120.

(6) Knight, Arthur. *The Liveliest Art, A Panoramic History of the Movies,* New York: A Mentor Book, New American Library, 1979. pp.16-17.

(7) Jacob, Lewis. *The Rise of the American Film, A Critical History,* New York: Harcourt, Brace & Co., 1939.

# SECTION II
# PART II
## THE EFFECTS OF TELEVISION

Watching television is a personal experience. One person might get frightened from watching a mystery, another might detach him/herself from the screen and view the program with a critical mind and thus control his/her reaction to the frightening scenes of the program. However, the fact is: television has a direct influence on its viewers. The degree of that effect is a function of the individual viewer, and the television material.

PART TWO examines the question of individual viewers' reactions to television, and the potential effects of television violence, sex, commercials, and news on the viewers.

CHAPTER VII:     THE EFFECTS OF TV & THE INDIVIDUAL VIEWER

CHAPTER VIII:    THE PROGRAMMING POLICY — THE TV CONTENT

CHAPTER IX:      VIOLENCE ON TV

CHAPTER X:       SEX ON TV

CHAPTER XI:      TV COMMERCIALS

CHAPTER XII:     TV NEWS

# Chapter VII

## THE EFFECTS OF TV &
## THE INDIVIDUAL VIEWER

*Effects of television on viewers are a result of a dynamic process in which the viewer and the television content interact. Since viewers are different from one another, the same television content can evoke different responses from different viewers.*

*Therefore, to study the effects of television, it becomes necessary to examine individual viewer's reactions to television, and the content of television.*

*This chapter focuses on the individual viewer's reactions to television.*

### INTRODUCTION:

There has been great concern regarding the possible harmful effects of television on the viewer, especially young children. Numerous studies attempted to study the cognitive, affective, behavioral and physical effects of watching television.

How does television affect a child's language development, creativity and imagination? Does watching violence in television make children more violent? Do commercials on television help develop a generation of non-discriminatory consumers? Do children adopt values and the style of life as portrayed in television programs? Do children of the television age learn more about world and national events than children of the radio age?

The preceding inquiries have been studied through research, observation and personal experience of parents, teachers, and students of communication. As early as the 1930's the Payne Fund Studies focused on similar questions pertaining to effects of motion pictures on youth. Comprehensive reports based on scientific research at Ohio State University by a number of leading psychologists and educators were published (1933-1936). (1) The studies showed that effects of motion pictures on young people is a matter that should be dealt with seriously.

Numerous studies followed which pointed to the fact that television does have cognitive, emotional, and physical effects, especially on children.

However, on the matter of accepting television in the lives of our children, researchers and the public in general are divided in three groups.

There are those who advocate turning off the set since the child's television experience is irrelevant and could be detrimental to the child's growing needs.

The second group holds the other side. They base their view on the premise that television entertains and informs the child. Questioning members of that group on the effects of television's portrayal of poor social values and violence, their answers point to an underlying understanding that children know "it is just on television." Questioning the indulgence of children in watching long hours of television, the answer is usually "the child will eventually outgrow it."

The third group feels that television is a fact of life. Children as well as parents in general like to watch it, yet at best it should be controlled. Within this group there are different views regarding how television can be controlled. One view states that control has to come from within the child. Accordingly, children have to be taught to become more selective in programs they watch and to be more critical in accepting what they see on TV. At the same time, parents, institutions, and civic groups have to work to improve the quality of programming to increase programs from which children choose. Another view advocates limiting veiwing time to certain programs, or to certain lengths, and/or time of the day.

Which of these three groups is right? To reach an answer to these questions, we will review in the following pages basic findings of researchers, parents, teachers, and observers on children's reactions to television.

## *Do Entertainment Programs Have Any Direct Influence on Viewers?*

Donna Woolfolk Cross, quoting Herbert Schiller, indicated that "One central myth dominates the world of fabricated fantasy: the idea that entertainment and recreation are value-free, have no point of view and exist outside . . . the social order." (2,p.85) She further pointed "Broadcasters uniformly deny that entertainment programs have any direct influence on how people think and behave." However, "Broadcasters will readily take credit for 'public interest' messages which they occasionally insert into entertainment programs." Documenting that claim, Cross reported that:

> Garry Marshall points proudly to the way shows such as *Happy Days* and *Laverne and Shirley* have helped push the idea of energy conservation: 'We are not saying buy this or do that. It's subliminal . . . We tie energy up with sex so viewers will listen!' (2,p.86)

She also cited Norman Lear saying "A half-hour documentary on seatbelts will make only so many converts, but have Archie Bunker or

Fonzie strap themselves in with a seatbelt and there will be a run on seatbelts everywhere." (2,p.87)

Marie Winn, the author of *The Plug-In Drug,* believes that "To a certain extent children's early television experiences will serve to dehumanize, to mechanize, to make less *real* the realities and relationships they encounter in life. For them, real events will always carry subtle echoes of the television world." (3,p.11) To illustrate this point, Winn reported on a twenty-year old who spent 20,000 hours of her life in front of the television set who said, "I didn't so much *watch* those shows when I was little, I let them watch over me . . . Now, I study them like the psychiatrist on his own couch looking hungrily for some clue inside the TV set to explain the person I have become." (3,p.11)

According to Schramm (4,p.75), most of children's learning from television is incidental. The child turns on the set not to learn, but to watch an entertaining program, to enjoy an exciting story, to watch a favorite performance, to laugh, or just to pass time.

The child's incidental learning from viewing television depends on: (1) his/her ability to learn, (2) his/her needs at the time of TV watching, (3) familiarity of the information presented on the screen, (4) how real the program appears to be, (5) degree of character identification, especially those the child favors, and (6) whether the information presented looks useful to the child.

The first two factors are common among all learning experiences. The rest of the factors have special significance to television.

TV presents a variety of unfamiliar experiences to the young child. Research has shown that learning from moving images is high when the information looks authentic. Since the child's limited experience does not provide him/her with a referral experience, the amount of incidental learning young children gain from television is high, especially when what they watch promises to be useful in their future social encounters. Moreover, when children establish an identity with characters, they tend to view the world with the eyes of that character. In many instances, television and motion picture stars started fads among young viewers ranging from the way they dress to the way they talk and behave.

The fact is that television is a powerful medium that affects the behavior of many viewers even when it is only trying to entertain. As Cross put it, "There must be millions of people who have learned, simply by watching crime dramas . . . that they have the right to remain silent when arrested . . . If this is true, then one must ask: What *else* may they have learned?" (2,p.87)

Sponsors are aware of the effect of messages explicitly or implicitly stated. Cross reported how sponsors emphasize hidden messages that can give a positive image to the product, such as the use of the product by the good guy and definitely not by the villain. For instance, "General Motors donated seven Chevy Camaros to *Mannix* on the condition that none would ever be driven by a heavy, and that when two crashed, the Chevy would never be the car that gets totaled." (2,p.89) Chrysler had a similar arrangement with the *Mod Squad*. Chrysler wanted what they called a "meaningful exposure" of their cars. A meaningful exposure will show the "side or the entire car, or the car driving into the camera with the name-plate on the screen." (2,p.89)

Content analysis of award winning commercials showed a tendency toward using middle class and upper-middle class settings in advertising products. (5) In all of the analyzed commercials, the product was associated or presented in a stream of beautiful visual imagery.

From the above, researchers, TV critics, educators, television producers and sponsors realize the direct influence that television has on its viewers. Evidence of television's influence is tremendous and beyond the scope of this chapter. If in doubt, one can ask two questions: First, why is it that advertising on television is in the billion-dollar range? Second, why is it extremely significant for our free democratic society to state that the air waves belong to the public?

## Factors Influencing the Effects of TV on Viewers

Effects of television on viewers are a result of a dynamic process in which the viewer and the television content interact. Since viewers are different from one another, the same television content can evoke different responses from different viewers. Watching television is a personal experience that differs with the individual. This is one reason why people have different interpretations of television effects. One person might get terrified from watching a supernatural demonic story, while another person can detach him/herself from the screen and view the program with a more critical eye.

Content of television is the second major factor in influencing the viewer. The content of television is more than a story being told, or information being communicated. It implicitly or explicitly advocates a style of life and a way of dealing with one's conflict with others. It also offers an interpretation of one's surroundings, and some of the national and interna-tional events. All of this is done with the intention of capturing the attention and interest of the viewer. Therefore, to understand the effects of television, the rest of this chapter will examine the question of the individual viewer's reaction to television, and the following chapter will focus on the content of television.

# THE INDIVIDUAL VIEWER

## *Reasons for Watching*

People turn on the television set for a variety of reasons: to be entertained, to kill time, to watch a news program, etc. Many turn on the set just out of habit, or just to keep some "noise" in the background. There are relatively few people who turn on the set to seek certain information. Public broadcasting and special informative or dramatic programs are the programs most watched by these few.

In general, children seldom turn on the set intentionally to seek information. However, they learn a variety of things from the programs they watch. This type of learning, as was mentioned earlier, is known as incidental learning.

Children's incidental learning from television is powerful and permanent, simply because it apparently meets their social needs: to find something they can talk about with their friends, or to know how to interact with each other. In many instances, children imitate the behavior of their favorite stars and heroes in the programs they watch.

To a great extent, children's felt needs determine how and what they view on television. However, felt needs are not necessarily what children really need to mature as effective social beings.

What they choose on television is also affected by what is available, and by their personal psychological and emotional state. For one child, a program can be frightening; to another, it could be just another program. Even some of the "family" programs to some children could be disturbing. For instance, a graduate student in one of my critical viewing classes said that *The Brady Bunch* was the most depressing program to her when she was young because she could see that her family simply was not as exciting as the Brady Bunch family. Dr. Fritz Redl, who was in charge of an experiment with disturbed and delinquent children in whose dormitories TV was available, reported that

> whereas for ordinary children the late-evening programs to be avoided would be violent and frightening ones, it was the "nice" and "sweet" programs showing loving parents and warm family relationships that caused this particular group of "problem children" to lie awake or to have bad dreams. These family programs reminded the children of what was lacking in their lives. And thus what would have been soothing (or at least innocuous) for most children was traumatic for these particular children because of their particular needs and backgrounds. (4,p.143)

67

Children's emotional and psychological state, lack of friends, lack of communication among family members and parents, reading difficulties, frustration from school work, and simply not knowing how to spend their time contribute to heavy viewing of TV and possibly more of its unwelcomed effects.

There is a difference in the effect that television has on a child who is cared for and guided to internalize a self-betterment attitude, from the effect on a child who is left in front of the television set for as long as he/she can take it.

A balanced diet of media exposure is needed for everyone, especially children. Children have to be encouraged to read newspapers, magazines, children's books, and attend children's theatre. In all of these activities, adults have to be examples of media literates and discriminating viewers of television.

## *Reality vs. Fantasy*

Faced with any situation, we bring in our past experience to help us interact with that situation. For a mature person, things which do not make sense in the light of past experience are viewed with a skeptical eye. For a child with no related experience to television material, he/she tends to accept what is presented as real. Since television conditions the viewer's perspective to accept the unreal as real, at least for the duration of the program, children with limited experience can easily confuse screen fantasy with reality. For a grown-up, King Kong is a huge dummy which was cleverly animated to present an exciting, adventurous, and unrealistic story. For the young child, King Kong is real. Sometimes even grown-ups can get caught in the world of television and confuse fantasy with real-life situations. Donna Cross reported that:

> Evidence of this confusion between reality and illusion grows daily. Trial lawyers, for example, complain that juries have become conditioned to the formulas of televised courtroom dramas . . .
>
> Television actors are frequently treated by their fans as though they actually were the characters they are paid to portray. (2,pp.221-222)

Confusing fantasy with reality does not happen only as an outcome of viewing entertainment programs. Americans, according to George Gerbner, have developed a "victim mentality." Larry Gross, a co-principal investigator of the Cultural Indicators Project with George Gerbner, reported that, "In instance after instance, adults who watch more television are likely to overestimate their chances of encountering violence, to overestimate the percentage of men employed in law enforcement and crime detection. They are more likely to reflect interpersonal mistrust, suggesting that 'most people' just look out for themselves, take advantage of others, and cannot be trusted." (6, p.21)

He further indicated that "adults who report that they 'frequently' watch evening police and crime programs also report that they have obtained dogs, guns, and locks for purposes of protection in greater proportion than those respondents who 'sometimes' or 'rarely/never' watch crime and police programs." (6, p.21)

## Total Absorption and Adult Discount

Many parents have reported that their children get totally absorbed while watching television. They get locked into what is happening on the screen, and become oblivious to anything else in their surroundings. Marie Winn described a trance-like state children experience while watching television. She said:

> The child's facial expression is transformed. The jaw is relaxed and hangs open slightly; the tongue rests on the front teeth (if there are any). The eyes have a glazed, vacuous look. Considering the infinite varieties of children's personalities and behavior patterns, there is a remarkable sameness of expression among television-watching children. Occasionally, they come out of the trance — when a commercial comes on, when the program ends, when they must go to the bathroom — but the obvious "snapping out" effect, as the face resumes a normal expression and the body returns to its normal state of semi-perpetual motion, only deepens the impression that the mental state of young children watching television is trancelike. There is certainly little indication that they are active and alert mentally. (3, p.14)

I think that children vary in their degree of absorption by television; however, they could get totally absorbed, and when the program is over, they re-enter the world of reality. The high level of excitement, especially at the end of the program as the story reaches its climax, usually in a last-minute rescue, is followed by a fade-out in music, sound, and action to leave the child in a state of withdrawal from an exciting fantasy world, and a sense of frustration to realize that his/her immediate surroundings are not as exciting as that of his/her heroes in televisionland. Some children can make this transition from the world of television to the world of reality faster than others. During that transition, crankiness and other unacceptable social behavior might be demonstrated in the form of verbal or physical violence. (3, p.21)

Adults, too, can get so absorbed in watching television. How many adults refuse to answer the telephone when their favorite program is on? And how many stay in front of television giving it their total attention, and paying none to other members of the family watching television with them in the same room?

Sometimes total adult absorption in television and motion pictures is translated into an overt behavior as indicated in the following three incidents. Although these incidents came from watching motion picture films, there is no reason to believe that the same could not happen in television.

1.  It was to my surprise to witness the gleeful audience reaction to a scene of killing in *Raiders of the Lost Ark*. After a dangerous chase, Indiana Jones was faced with a huge Arab waving his sword demonstrating his skill with it. To put an end to a very dangerous challenge, Indiana Jones pulled out his gun and shot the man. The audience applauded the act. Unable to comprehend how people could applaud the killing of a man, ten days later, I repeated my visit to the same theatre to witness the same reaction from another audience. The possible explanation for such a phenomenon is that the audience was so absorbed by the fast-moving action in the film that members of the audience seemingly identified with Indiana Jones. Not knowing what to do if they were in that situation, they broke into laughter at the surprise action of their hero.

2.  In the second incident, a mother of three children got totally absorbed in watching *Jaws*. Her state of fear was translated into a state of anxiety. On returning home from the theatre, she awkwardly asked her husband to look underneath the bed to see if anyone was hiding. Needless to say, the enjoyable family days at the beach were limited to the children playing out of the water.

3.  In the third incident, an anesthesiologist had to stay away from the operating room for two weeks after watching *Psycho*. In her words, "I could not erase from my mind the image of the shower-water washing away the blood of the victim into the drain. Dissolving the image of the drain opening into the wide-opened eye of the dead woman was just too much to forget."

The problem with total absorption in the televisionland is more serious with children in their growing years than grownups. Children suffering from annoying problems might find the television world a more comfortable place to be in, and the more they watch, the more they look for more, and thus become heavy viewers and addicted to television. Childhood is the time they have to deal with real-life situations and real family interaction to discover themselves and to know the world around them. Children need to get to know people, to develop friendship, to question and to find satisfying answers to their inquiries, to learn how to express themselves and how to communicate with others, to learn to read and to write, to practice problem solving, and to experience a fulfilling and a satisfying social life. The more they get absorbed in television, the less time they have to experience an active life, and to develop communication skills they need for an effective and rewarding life. No wonder that children who are heavy viewers of television do not do that well in school.

As grownups, we practice what is known as "adult discount." (1,p.42) Adult discount is a mechanism we apply so that we don't get totally absorbed and emotionally involved in a television program, to guard us against excess emotional and psychological reaction to exciting stories and frightening scenes.

Two things are needed to develop this skill. First, understanding of television's methods of persuasion, and second, constantly reminding ourselves that what we are watching is not real. Stepping out of the role of a passive watcher to an objective viewer examining how the program is structured to convey its messages strengthens the adult discount skill.

Children need to develop that skill. They also are in need of guidance to develop other interesting activities they can perform during their leisure time. To meet both needs, adults have to set up a model of discriminating viewers who understand the medium, and can engage themselves in self-rewarding activities during their free time.

# REFERENCES

1. Charters, W.W. *Motion Pictures & Youth, A Summary,* New York: The Macmillan Company, 1935.

2. Cross, Donna Woolfolk. *Mediaspeak, How TV Makes Up Your Mind,* New York: A Mentor Book, 1983.

3. Winn, Marie. *The Plug-In Drug, Television, Children, and the Family,* Revised Edition, New York: Penguin Books, 1985.

4. Schramm, Wilbur, et. al. *Television in the Lives of Our Children,* Stanford, California: Stanford University Press, 1961.

5. Hefzallah, Ibrahim & Maloney, W. Paul. "Content Analysis of TV Commercials," *Monograph,* Fairfield University Library, Fairfield, Conn. 1975.

6. Gross, Larry. "Television and Violence," in *Television Awareness Training,* Ben Logan (Ed.), Abingdon/Nashville, 1979.

# Chapter VIII
# THE PROGRAMMING POLICY
———
# THE TV CONTENT

*The second major factor influencing the effects of television on the viewers is the content of television.*

*Television content is determined by the programming policy adopted by the networks, network affiliates, independent stations, and public broadcast television stations.*

*Therefore, studying television's programming policy and practice can help explain the existing television programs on both open and cable broadcast channels.*

Programmers of television stations aim at attracting as many viewers as possible to watch their stations. This entails knowing *who* is watching *what* on *what channel* and at *what time.* It also entails knowing the sequence of programs on the competing channels. Usually programs with the same ambience follow each other in an attempt to keep the audience of that type of programs from shifting to a competing channel.

The "who" aspect of that four-fold question focuses on audience demographics. The "what", the "channel", and the "time" determine which program will be shown on a certain channel and at what time after taking into consideration the demographics of the audience as well as what is being presented on competing channels.

To understand this process it is essential to understand the television channel system and the interrelationships between affiliated and competing channels.

## *Introduction: The Television Broadcasting System*

Open circuit broadcasts are conventional broadcasts transmitted over an assigned frequency to a given area. Standard television receivers can tune in those broadcasts. The range of open-circuit transmission covers a radius of about fifty miles. The range of transmission depends on the power of the station measured in kilowatt, geographical contours, and other factors. The signal must be amplified and rebroadcast if it is to be received beyond that radius.

The number of television channels is less than the number of FM radio channels, and it is far less than AM radio channels in a given area. This is because of the following factors:

1.  The television broadcasting spectrum is limited under present rules. All in all, there are twelve VHF channels. The VHF band consists of a low band, channels 2 through 6, and a high band, channels 7 through 13. The UHF band has seventy channels, channels 14 through 83.

2.  The television signal spans a band of six megacycles in width, while a hundred AM radio broadcast channels can be fitted within a bandwidth of one megacycle of frequency, and only five FM channels can be fitted into a band width of one megacycle.

3.  According to the FCC rules, television stations operating on the same channel must be from 155 to 220 miles apart, depending on their frequency and the geographical location. Stations operating on adjacent channels have to be from 55 to 60 miles apart. (1,p.9) (Notice that channel 4 and channel 5 are separated by 4 megacycles on the broadcasting spectrum; channel 4 operates on 66-72 megacycle band, and channel 5 operates on 76-82 megacycle band. This makes it possible to have channels 4 and 5 operating from the same city such as WNBC/4 and WNEW/5 in New York City.)

At present, most open-circuit broadcasting is transmitted on the VHF bands (2-13) which permits a total of eight to nine stations reception at the same time in one location without interference.

About ten years after the VHF frequencies had been assigned, another set of seventy UHF channels were found to be feasible for television broadcasting. However, most of commercial television broadcasting today is on the VHF band. The FCC has made it mandatory that all television receivers manufactured after April 30, 1964, must be capable of receiving UHF signals. (2,p.5) Before that date, special adapters were available to be used on home receivers for receiving UHF signals. At present, a large percentage of the public tunes in stations operating on the VHF band more than tuning in UHF stations for the following reasons.

1.  The majority of UHF stations are non-commercial stations broadcasting serious types of programs. Being habituated to television as mainly an entertaining medium and that educational programs cannot be fun, the majority of the audience turns to entertaining programs on commercial channels on the VHF band.

2.  Most of the homes are equipped with VHF antennas only. The wire loop supplied by the manufacturer with the set permits good reception of the UHF band if the receiver is not far away from the transmitting tower. (This situation is improved if the household subscribes to cable television basic service.)

## Allocation of TV Channels for Non-Commercial Uses

In 1927 the Congress enacted the first regulatory law governing radio transmission ". . . the radio spectrum belonged to the public and that a broadcaster acquired no ownership rights in a frequency when granted a license." This was continued in the 1934 Act creating the Federal Communications Commission and its subsequent revisions.

The FCC has adopted the following policy regarding the distribution of television channels:

1. Provision of at least one television service to all parts of the country, and at least one station to each community; then if possible, providing a choice of at least two television services to all parts of the country and providing each community with at least two stations.

2. Provision of at least one non-commercial educational television channel in every major community and educational center. This it could not do, but it did explicitly recognize the special needs of many primarily educational centers. (1,p.10)

In making the final allocations of more than two thousand channels, it reserved 12 percent of all channel assignments for non-commercial purposes — a total of 242, which was increased to 274 channels (1,p1) — 182 on the UHF band and 92 on the VHF band. Moreover, in 1966, "a revised table of channel assignments was adopted for UHF, containing many more educational assignments than before. The new table contains altogether over 615 educational TV assignments in the mainland states, more than a third of all channels assignments." (3,A6) At present, there are approximately 114 VHF and 176 UHF noncommercial channels in operation. (3,A2)

## The Advent of Cable Television

Cable television has changed the problem of television channel scarcity. New cable television installations have the capacity of 36+ channels. It is required to carry all local channels and public television channels in addition to importing distant channels. Public access channels are also required by law. Cable television has turned the limited broadcasting system into a much broader spectrum allowing for clear reception whether the channel is on the UHF band or the VHF band. This feature made it possible for the least powerful public television stations operating on the UHF band to be received clearly in cable television homes.

Although the scarcity problem has been minimized, the network programming policy based on competition between few channels received by the public still dominates the television industry. The bottom line of this policy is to attract the largest number of audience to a channel and to keep that number watching as long as possible.

## *The Networks Programming Dominence*

Approximately 72% (seventy-two percent) of television stations operating in the U.S. are affiliated with one of the three networks. (3,A2) Although affiliated stations are not required by law to carry network programming, yet seventy percent of the programming carried by the affiliates is supplied by the networks. The rest of the time is devoted to local origination including news, local sports, public affairs programs, and occasional movies and syndicated video programs.

There are three reasons behind the popularity and programming dominance of the networks. First, local affiliates simply cannot match their resources to that of the networks to produce or acquire first-run programs of the same quality provided by the networks. Second, local stations have to allocate funds to produce programs serving the interest of their local communities, and to acquire syndicated programs to personalize themselves. Third, networks pay the affiliates carrying network programs about 30% of the stations' potential advertising revenues if the stations were to program the time period themselves. (4,p.2-26) In addition, affiliates can sell time for short advertising messages during station breaks in a network program. Therefore, it is a relief for affiliates to fill seventy percent of their broadcast time with network programs.

Strategic program planning is a necessity for local independent stations to survive. In this planning, analysis of networks and local affiliates programs is made. Usually, local independent stations counter program the networks and their affiliates. Counter programming is the scheduling of one type of program that has a different audience appeal from other programs on other stations. For instance, on weekdays from 7:00 - 7:30 p.m. the three networks broadcast news. Independent New York VHF television channels: WNEW Channel 5, WOR Channel 9, and WPIX channel 11 broadcast *Mash, 100,000 Pyramid,* and *The Jeffersons* respectively during that time slot.

In addition to counter programming, local dependent stations attempt to personalize their on-the-air presence. This is usually achieved through: (a) choice of certain programs for certain time slots, (b) developing a public image of their on-the-air personalities especially news, sports, and weather broadcasters, and (c) developing a positive civic image through broadcasting of editorials and reporting on matters of concern to the citizens of the local community.

Similar to network affiliates, independent local stations' local production is also limited to news, local sports, and public affairs programs. Syndicated programs and movies are the prime sources for the rest of local independent stations programming activities. For example, on Wednesday, January 16, 1985, the three VHF New York independent channels WNEW, WOR, and WPIX broadcast between 6:00 to 12:00 p.m. five, three, and two and a half hours of syndicated programs respectively. WNEW had one hour of news; WOR had one half hour of news, and two and a half hours of sports; and WPIX had one hour and a half of news, and a two-hour movie.

Syndicated programs fall under two categories: (a) new or first-run syndications, and (b) rerun syndicated programs which are tape copies of programs run on the networks. Naturally the cost of acquiring first-run programs is higher than that of leasing rerun syndicated programs. Accordingly, to minimize the operation cost of local independent stations, more reruns are shown.

From the above analysis of programming techniques practiced by both network affiliates and independent local stations, the dominance of networks, in terms of what is shown at what time and on which channel, is clear. Networks set the type and programming pattern of both the independent stations and the networks affiliates (4, chapter 2). This dominance will be put to rigorous tests as new video telecommunications technologies invade homes and get accepted by the public. The new telecommunication technology will increase the availability of delivery channels and programming systems, and thus will decrease the number of viewers available at any time to watch network television. For instance, it is common in new cable television installations to have close to 24 channels for a basic fee. Special channels, such as movie channels, are made available to the subscribing household at an additional charge. Satellite transmission has already provided centralized cost-effective distribution of programs to cable operators, and broadcast stations. When satellite receivers are marketed at an affordable price to the public, homes will be able to receive direct broadcast from satellites.

The integration of a personal computer keyboard, the home television set, and the telephone or cable lines opens a new and challenging utilization of the home television set. Home television sets are evolving into a telecommunication screen via which people receive a variety of programs, play games, retrieve information, receive college credits, and improve their standard of living. These viable and new uses of television will decrease the number of networks' potential audience when the public accepts the new technology and learns how to use it efficiently. Since it will take time for the public to achieve that status, programming techniques practiced at present will be with us for a few years to come.

# PROGRAMMING OBJECTIVES AND DECISIONS

The main objective of a station's programming policy is to attract the largest number of viewers and keep them watching that station as long as possible. Television is not in the business to entertain. Its business is selling the presence of an audience to the advertiser. The more people watch a show, the more income is generated from advertising. As it is often said, "It is the audience and not programs or air time that the networks really sell." (5,6,7)

To increase the size of the audience, the program has to appeal to and capture the interest of a large segment of the population. Its programming policy, therefore, is to provide images and sound that appeal to the imagination and fantasy of those who turn on the set searching for a happy and relaxing time. Very seldom a viewer will encounter a thought-provoking program on commercial channels, especially during prime time. Documentaries have disappeared from commercial prime-time television because programmers believe that documentaries tend to drive viewers away from the network. (7,p.29)

The structure of entertainment programs is simple and relies on naive characterization and stereotypes. Violence and sex are two ingredients believed to make programs more exciting to watch. To present a variety of shows in one evening, most of the programs are tailored to a half- or one-hour slots and thus having no room for the development of good characterization and convincing story lines, nor for experimentation of innovative ideas. Once a program succeeds as an audience getter, similar programs are produced imitating that program such as in the cases of *Dallas* and *Dynasty,* and the numerous police and detective shows. In other instances, a new program is built around a popular secondary character of a successful program. For example, when *All In The Family* became the most popular show in America, "CBS took the character of Archie Bunker's acerbic cousin, Maude Finley, and featured her in her own series. The success of that show led to the spinning-off of Maude's maid, Florida, into her own series, *Good Times.* The Bunkers' next-door neighbors, an upwardly mobile black family, the Jeffersons, were also given their series." (7,pp.31-32)

The fear of experimenting with new ideas is due to the fear of losing audience in the event that the program does not appeal to the viewers. If station A loses some of its audience to station B, it actually means increasing the revenues of station B. Networks and stations are very conscious of a phenomenon known as the "audience flow." If an audience of television station A became disappointed with a program and tunes in station B, the chance will be that they will stay in tune with channel B for the following program. In other words, a failure program affects the program that follows in the schedule. Since programs are designed to deliver the audience to the next commercial, maintaining audience flow is a necessity. Usually programs with the same general ambience follow each other. For an audience interested in this type of programs, the first program in the evening delivers them to the second, and the second delivers them to the third, and so on.

## Ratings and Demographics

Knowing what people like to watch cannot be left to guess work. This is why the ratings, measuring the number of the audience watching a program, are an intricate element in programming decisions. It is also important to know the type of an audience watching the show. Sometimes, the ratings might be high, yet the show is cancelled because of the audience demographics, as reported by Greenfield,

> Throughout television history, popular shows have been cancelled not just because the ratings have been low, but because the audience has not been sufficiently attractive economically. In 1967 *Gunsmoke* was saved from cancellation only through the personal intervention of CBS founder and chairman of the board, William S. Paley. Despite the program's high ratings its audience was deemed too old, too rural. Even when the long-running western was cancelled in 1975, it was still one of the thirty most popular shows in America. (7,p.29)

Research on ratings and demographics is conducted by commercial companies. In this research, a sample of the population is polled to measure the number and the make-up — demographics — of an audience of a program, and the channels being viewed.

Techniques and methods of polling the public vary depending on information sought, and facilities available to the researcher. Three methods are usually used. (8)

1. **The telephone coincidental method.** In this method a preselected sample of the population is called by phone and asked if they have their television set on; if so, what channel are they watching, and how many members of the family are watching. Although this method is economical to the researcher, the interviewers are likely to be annoyed. In addition telephone calls can not be made early in the morning or late at night. Accordingly, the survey is limited.

2. **The diary method.** In this method, a diary is given to a sample of preselected households. The diary is kept next to the television set. The family members are requested to record programs they watch and on

which channels. When returned to the research firm, the results are tabulated. Usually, the diary contains information about the viewer.

3. **The electronic recorder method.** In this method an electronic recorder is connected to the television set of the participating household. It records the time the set was on, the channel the set was tuned to, all the channel switching, and the duration of each channel received. The information is collected automatically from the set, and can be communicated by wire directly to the researcher's recording center. Since it does not show whether anyone was really watching, or the composition of the audience during the time the set was on, in some studies, the family members are asked to keep a log indicating persons viewing as well as programs viewed.

The major audience research companies are Nielsen (9) and Arbitron (10). Both companies compete in local markets, however, Nielsen ratings are the yardstick used at the network level. (11)

Two commonly used terms in reporting the ratings are: "Share of Audience" and "Rating." "Share of the Audience" refers to the percentage of households watching a program to the total number of households watching television at that time. "Rating" refers to the percentage of households watching a program to the total number of television households, whether they have their television on or not.

Since the public in general turns the television set to watch television and not specific programs, ratings are actually indications of what the public dislikes least and not what the public wants. (11,p.257) Ratings, however, determine which programs will stay on the air, which will be cancelled, the place of the program in the broadcast schedule, and eventually the cost of advertising on that program.

Ratings are also considered by television producers. Programs with high ratings are imitated. As a result we get repetitive and similar programs on various television channels.

Those responsible for programming claim, however, that they are giving the people what they want. As a former network vice-president reported, "It's not what I personally like that matters. What you ask is 'Will thirty million Americans watch this?' I'm not programming for my friends or your friends. I'm programming for people — people who are less educated than I am, who traveled less, who read fewer books." (7,p.32)

Feeding the public the same diet of programs, and given the tendency of the public to watch television no matter what is on, there is no way of really knowing what the public wants. However, if the public's critical viewing skills are developed, television programmers have to take into consideration a different public taste.

# THE CONTENT OF TELEVISION

In studying the programming policy of television stations, it was indicated that the prime concern of a television station is to attract as many viewers as possible, and to hold them in front of the television receiver the longest time possible. The reason is the underlying fact that commercial television is not in the business of entertaining or educating the public, it is in the business of selling the presence of an audience to the sponsors.

The sponsors in turn are not interested in the story line, or the degree of realism of the program, but more in projecting beautiful images of people and places, and exciting action to keep the audience in front of the set until the commercial break. Robert MacNeil expressed this practice of programming when he said, "The object is to disconnect the audience from uncomfortable realities, to lull it on a scene of gentle inconsequence — and then to sell it deodorant." (12)

Television is a hungry medium for talent and material. In spite of the vast amount of television production in this country, still a large percentage of independent stations and network affiliates telecast reruns of sitcom programs which were previously carried by networks.

Satellite transmission and cable television companies brought specialized and pay channels to the homes. Studying the programming of the pay channels, one can easily see that the pay channels reserve a limited number of box-office successful movies and a large number of mediocre and low budget movies characterized by graphic violence, sex, and verbal vulgarity.

A successful program on commercial or pay television stations is a program that attracts a large audience. Once a program succeeds, similar programs are tailored using the same formula. This explains, as previously indicated, the Norman Lear's series in the early seventies, and the large number of films broadcast by pay television channels focusing on the sexual fantasy of the adolescent, such as *Spring Break, Porky I,* and *Porky II.* It also explains the similarities between game shows in which contestants compete to acquire beautiful possessions: cars, refrigerators, paid trips to some exotic places, etc.

Even news programs have not escaped the same dilemma. News programs are not only designed to give news, but to make news programs appealing to the majority of the audience. Teasers inviting the audience to tune in later in the evening, or to stay tuned-in to the end of the news program are common practice.

To stay in business, television has to appeal to a large section of the population. Television programs can be appealing if they have a good story line, well-cherished values, good acting, and a smooth convincing presentation of the story. To do this, talented writers, actors, directors, editors, and producers with a vision and a sense of commitment to the public as well as to the visual art of television are needed. This will not only drive up the cost of production to astronomical figures, but it will not produce enough programs to feed the long hours of television broadcasting. Therefore, the solution adopted by commercial television is to produce a few quality programs and a bulk of relatively low-budget, and sensory appealing programs.

Sex, fast action, visually graphic violence, psychedelic visual effects, verbal vulgarity, and fear-evoking situations are financially feasible programming techniques. As a result, there is an overabundance of sex — implicit and explicit; graphic and verbal violence; frightening scenes; visual dreamlike effects, such as in music video; and fast action of people, cars, airplanes, and twenty-first century gadgets and weapons. All of these devices are used to present mediocre stories that fail to instill self-redeeming values, especially in the young, and a critical misinterpretation of the world and of reality.

# REFERENCES

1. Powell, John Walker. *Channels of Learning, The Story of Educational Television,* Washington D.C.: Public Affairs Press, 1962. p.9.

2. Gordon, George. *Educational Television,* New York: The Center for Applied Research in Education, Inc., 1965. p.5.

3. *Broadcasting Cablecasting Yearbook 1985,* Washington D.C.

4. Robb, Scott H. *Television/Radio Age, Communications Coursework,* Communications Research Institute 78-79 Edition.

5. Logan, Ben, "They Started the Revolution Without Me," in *Television Awareness Training, The Viewer's Guide for Family & Community,* B. Logan (Ed.) Abingdon/Nashville 1979. pp.7-11.

6. Liebert, Diane, "Television Advertising and Values," in *Television Awareness Training, The Viewer's Guide for Family & Community,* B. Logan (Ed.) Abingdon/Nashville 1979. pp.43-48.

7. Greenfield, Jeff. *Television — The First Fifty Years,* New York: Crescent Books, 1981. p.29.

8. Kleppner, Otto. *Advertising Procedure,* 6th Edition, Englewood Cliffs, N.J.: Prentice-Hall, 1974. p.153.

9. For more information, A.C. Nielsen makes available, free of charge, four brochures to educators by writing to Promotion Manager, A.C. Nielsen Company, Nielsen Plaza, Northbrook, Illinois 60062. Those brochures are:
   a. *Everything You've Always Wanted to Know About TV Ratings*
   b. *The Nielsen Ratings in Perspective*
   c. *The Diversified Services of A.C. Nielsen Company*
   d. Annual Nielsen Report on Televsion

10. For more information, Arbitron Ratings Company makes available, free of charge, an information package to educators by writing to Arbitron Ratings, 1350 Avenue of the Americas, N.Y., N.Y. 10019. The package includes the following items which provide interesting information on TV ratings:
    a. *Arbitron Ratings Today*
    b. *Portfolio of Services*
    c. *Description of Methodology*
    d. *Television Meter Service*

11. "Ratings," in *Television Awareness Training, The Viewer's Guide for Family & Community,* B. Logan (Ed.) Abingdon/Nashville 1979. pp.257-258.

12. Quoted by Cross, Donna Woolfolk. *Mediaspeak, How TV Makes Up Your Mind,* A Mentor Book, 1984. p.85.

# Chapter IX

# VIOLENCE ON TELEVISION

*Television programs that generate a great deal of concern among parents and educators are those that contain scenes of violence. Research has indicated a modest correlation between television violence and aggressive behavior of children. Viewed in the light of millions of children who watch television for long hours every day, especially those who use it to escape their personal, familial, school, and friendship problems, there is a tremendous cause for being concerned.*

*Even if scientific evidence does not totally support the claim that violence in television teaches children to commit violent acts, there is more evidence that television violence could be harmful to the proper upbringing of children.*

TV programs that generate a great deal of concern among parents and educators are those that contain scenes of violence. The concern about visualized violence goes back to the dawn of motion pictures. In the famous Payne Fund Studies, a critical content analysis of 1500 movie titles was conducted. The concern about the overabundence of violence in those movies was best expressed in the following:

> We agree wholly with the need for an unshackled screen, for the treatment of crime *as a social fact.* But that treatment, and the treatment of any social fact, demands proper emphasis. Unfortunately, however, the motion-picture screen has given an emphasis to crime and violence which would characterize an individual as abnormal if he were thus preoccupied. This preoccupation crowds out pictures dealing with other fundamental problems of living. It makes the screen almost barren of pictures of beauty, idealism, and imaginative charm. Further, while there can be no approval of a screen which entirely shuts off fundamental facts from the public, yet one can get these facts from a variety of other sources, and frequently in much better form. Therefore, while we have no desire to exclude the fundamental and adequate treatment of crime from

the screen, we do not wish to accord it the emphasis which it receives in the lives of normal, intelligent people. (1,p.122)

In a more recent study of 100 hours of television programs, it was reported by Schramm that:

For the most part, ... the children's hour on commercial television (4-9:00 p.m.) is a succession of fast-moving, exciting fantasy, leavened with broad humor and a considerable amount of romantic interest. It is extremely violent. Shootings and sluggings follow each other interminably. More than half the one-hundred hours are given over to programs in which violence plays an important part. (2,p.139)

More recently, the public's concern has been reflected in congressional hearings and massive studies on the effect of TV violence, especially on children. All of the studies focused on potential harm of TV violence on children. However, there is not a simple answer as to whether viewing TV violence will make children more aggressive or violent. Commenting on research on television violence, Robert Singer stated that

There are more published studies that find that TV is linked to aggression than there are published studies that do not find such a connection. The studies that do establish a connection find a rather modest one, with it being unlikely that more than 4 or 5% of children's aggression can be attributed to television viewing. (3,p.57)

The reason for not having a clear-cut answer is that the effect of TV is an outcome of not only the content and how it is portrayed, but most importantly, of the children themselves, their interpersonal relationship with their families, friends, teachers, the family atmosphere, and how the children are treated by members of their families. In the words of Dr. L.Z. Freedman,

The intensity and psychic significance of the child's response to television is the *reciprocal* of the satisfactions he gains in the milieu of his family, school, and friends. One would predict that the less intelligent, the most disturbed youngsters, and those having the poorest relationship with their families and peers would be most likely to immerse themselves in televiewing as escape or stimuli. Intelligent, relatively stable youngsters in reasonably harmonious homes would be comparatively unaffected by it. (2,p.157)

Schramm underscored the same idea saying that, "Children with satisfactory interpersonal relationships . . . are least likely to be harmed by any experience with television." (2,p.157) However, if a child is psychologically and socially maladjusted with a tendency for rebellion, he might use a television crime as a "model" for his rebellion.

The reader might recall a few unfortunate incidents in which a young person committed a violent act to indicate later that he/she got the idea of that act from a television show. The same belief is held by Robert Singer:

> Working-class children, minority children, unpopular children, and children doing poorly in school seem to be the ones more susceptible to imitating the aggression that they see on television. This may be partly because they watch more hours and are exposed to more television violence, but it is also for other reasons . . . The direction of causation is not simple, since highly aggressive children have a preference for watching programs high on violence. Television may or may not contribute to their aggressive behavior, but their aggressive nature does play a major role in what they choose to watch. (3,p.57)

From the above, it seems that there is a modest correlation between TV violence and aggressive behavior of children. Viewed in the light of millions of children who watch television for long hours every day, especially those who use it to escape their personal, familial, school and friendship problems, there is a tremendous cause for being concerned.

Larry Gross best expressed the above idea, "While scientific caution requires us to proceed carefully in drawing conclusions from the wealth of data and evidence that has been accumulated, many patterns seem well-established. (4)

The harmful effects of television violence really go beyond teaching children to be violent. So even if scientific evidence does not totally support the claim that violence in television teaches children to commit violent acts, there is more evidence, as well as common sense, that television violence could be harmful to the proper upbringing of children. In discussing learning and television violence, Alberta E. Siegel wrote:

> We are left with evidence which gives some cause for concern, plus common sense which tells us that any activity occupying so many hours in a person's life must have lasting significance for him. Both the evidence and common sense converge to suggest that TV's continuous preoccupation with stereotyped violent conflict and its resolution through violence can hardly be constructive and healthful for the child viewer. (5,p.236)

## REASONS FOR CONCERN

### *First: Overabundance of Violent Acts*

There is overabundance of violent acts on the screen, as Alberta Siegel put it: "TV entertainment is dominated by themes of violence." (5) "It has often been noted that by the time the average American child graduates from high school, he will have seen more than 13,000 violent deaths, all of them on television." (4)

In the Cultural Indicator Project conducted by George Gerbner, Larry Gross and associates, violence was defined as "the overt expression of physical force, with or without a weapon, against self or others; compelling action against one's will on pain of being hurt or killed, or actually hurting or killing." (4) In "Violence Profile" of 1977, in that project, the researchers noted that:

> the percentage of programs containing violence has ranged in the nine years of our study from 80 to 90 percent. In the fall of 1977 it was 75.5 percent. The rate of violent episodes per hour rose to a record high of 9.5 in 1976; in 1977 it was a typical 6.7 episodes per hour. The percentage of characters involved in violence has ranged from 56 to 75 percent, and averages at 63 percent over the last nine years.
>
> Weekend morning programs, the period referred to in the industry as the "kidvid ghetto," contain the highest rate of violent actions. In 1977 there were scenes of violence in nine out of ten programs at a rate of 16 per hour. (4,p.20)

A single analysis of prime-time programs in the summer of 1985 showed high incidences of violence especially in music video programs. (6) Moreover, the sheer amount of violence in children's Saturday morning programs was shocking.

## Second: Misrepresentation of Real Violence

TV violence is a misrepresentation of real violence in many aspects:

(1) TV violence is more frequent than real violence. A child watches 115,000 acts of television violence by the time he/she is 18 years of age. As a result of a heavy diet of television violence, heavy viewers of television overestimate the actual occurrence of violent crime in America. In a study of people's expectation to be a victim of a serious crime, heavy viewers overestimated that chance. Also, they are usually afraid of being hurt by others. (4,p.21)

(2) TV drama deals mostly with crimes that are the easiest for the poor and disadvantaged to commit, and aggression is usually presented as a solution to a complicated problem — the elimination of the maladjusted. White collar crimes, which are on the rise (7) such as price-fixing, violations of work safety, and misleading advertising are seldom presented in television drama. (8,p.113)

(3) TV violence spares the audience the agony of the victim, and the

conscious turmoil of the killer. Effects of violent acts on relatives and loved ones of the victim are usually implied but not explicitly portrayed. After all, in thirty minutes or sixty minutes, how much can be presented and still keep the audience tuned in?

## Third: Solution to Conflict

Violence on TV is usually presented as the solution to conflict among people, and usually good guys commit murders to eliminate the "criminal." Continuous presentation of violence as an answer to conflict can teach young people that conflicts can be solved through aggression, and not through communication, recognition, and respect of differences among people. Larry Gross reported on two surveys conducted by the Cultural Indicator Project in which children were asked, "How often is it all right to hit someone if you are mad at them?" It was found out that "heavy viewers of television, more often than light viewers of television, responded that it is "almost alright to hit someone." (4,p.20) Singer believes that:

> It is more important to look into what television teaches children about how individuals, society, and nations handle conflict, than at whether or not it contributes to individual acts of aggression. Perhaps television's most detrimental aspect as far as aggression is concerned, is the tendency to portray violence as the usual outcome when people are in conflict. (3,p.59)

## Fourth: Mythical Heroes

The hero of violent television drama is a mythical person, usually a single male who is skilled with knives, guns, Karate, and who has his way with beautiful women. He is usually a person who can go through extreme physical punishment and get out of car crashes, gun fights, and fist fights unharmed to appear in another episode doing exactly the same. A hit on the head that might cause him a severe concussion, which in real life would necessitate months to be cured, the television hero somehow endures, and gets up to resume severe fighting and wins by eliminating the opponents. There is not much difference between Mannix, 007 (with a license to kill), Superman and Magnum. They all represent a mythical, unbeatable hero who takes sides to fight the forces of evil and triumph with violent acts.

## Fifth: Sensory Overkill

In one of the early film classics, *Intolerance,* the battle scene was one of the first violent scenes in motion picture history. Soldiers were beheaded, swords penetrated bodies, people were pushed off a high wall. A great deal of special effects went into the making of that scene to make it convincing. However, as gory as they appeared, blood was seldom shown.

89

Today, movie and television producers of violent drama have outdone themselves. Looking for new tricks, and achieving a degree of realism, the audience is shown acts of body destruction in close-up shots — throats being cut, bodies being stabbed, brains being blasted out, bodies on fire, someone being killed underwater — and as more special effects and stunts are mastered, more graphic and gory violence will be presented.

In doing so, excitement through violent acts is emphasized. Yet, as was mentioned earlier, it is still sanitized, keeping the audience as an observer. These two conditions result in desensitizing people to the agony of others, and for children it could terrify them, especially as they develop their cognitive ability to comprehend the dimension of physical harm.

### Sixth: Fear and Suspense

Violence, as was mentioned earlier, is often used as an element of excitement in TV drama. However, violence by itself cannot sustain the interest of the audience. If however, violence is interwoven in a suspenseful structure of events, an audience can be more easily captivated.

Children and young people in general love excitement. A visitor to an amusement park can witness children's and young people's attraction to thrilling rides, and exciting ventures through a "fun house" ride. However, one has to remember that they usually seek excitement and not fear, and that the line between fear and excitement is a fine line, as Schramm noted, "... many writers on children's emotional development have observed (that) there is a fine line between excitement and fear. Fear may leave scars; excitement is relatively harmless unless it gets out of control." (2,p.149)

Children differ in how much and in what type of excitement they can handle without losing control. For one child, a scene might be more frightening than to another child. There are five TV situations which seem most likely to frighten children. These situations are:

1. When harm threatens a character with whom they identify closely or to whom they feel especially attached. This is particularly true when the harm is physically more direct, such as that inflicted by a knife, or if its effect is graphically portrayed, such as in the incident of a gun shot causing a sudden impact and a body bleeding and destruction. (2,p.148)

2. Situations which remind the child of his/her own real-life fears. In many horror and suspenseful violent dramas, scenes are relatively dark, shadows are exaggerated and depicted through a flash of lighting or through harsh directional lighting. Sound could be as frightening, such as the sound of creaking floors under the heavy footsteps of the unmerciful

villain, evil music, and exaggerated sound effects. All of these are trade marks of horror and violent programs, and they depict situations similar to those when a child is alone and frightened by shadows playing on the wall of his/her bedroom, and strange noises coming from within or outside the child's bedroom on a stormy thundering night. (2,p.149)

3. The unexpected and violent situations. To keep the audience captivated, many times the television maker surprises the audience with a dangerous and unexpected situation such as removing the bed cover before the heroine goes to sleep to face a huge poisonous snake poised to attack the surprised and horrified actress, or walking down a dark staircase to investigate a strange noise in a basement to be faced by a masked intruder holding a large shiny kitchen knife. In such instances, the audience is not prepared to handle such a dangerous surprise and they are led into a state of panic, especially if they indentify with the actor. Philip, an eleven-year-old, expressed his fear when watching *Hallowe'en*. He said,

> I was scared by *Hallowe'en*. This guy was insane and escaped from an institution and he was going in this house and trying to cut up these girls. The scariest part was when this girl was trying to make sure that he wasn't there and he jumped out of the closet. (9,p.28)

4. Complicated dangerous situations in which the favorite character looks like he has been trapped with no possible way out, such as being trapped in a burning house, or inside a sound-proof chamber as deadly gas seeps through openings in the wall. In many of these instances, the escape of the hero is unrealistic, and playing to what is known as the last-minute rescue will prolong the state of fear a child experiences. As children mature, they will come to know that everything is going to be all right, and somehow their favorite character will be able to escape that danger or be rescued. In such a case, this fear is diverted to concentrating on how the director will get the hero out of that danger. If the escape is logical and reasonable, the incident will prove to be just an unharmful exciting experience. If it does not seem logical, they might ridicule the simplistic and naive structure of the program.

5. Graphic portrayal of body destruction. Searching for exciting images, television producers outdo themselves in presenting graphic portrayal of violent acts. Heads being cut off, bullets bursting the chest of a victim, brains blown out, a strangled victim as he drops dying on the ground with tongue hanging out and eyes extruding from their sockets, fountains of blood emerging from the body of a victim, limbs being cut and floating in water, and the list can go on and on.

Children can really get scared from watching graphic portrayals of violence. Marisian, an eleven-year-old child reported, "I was scared when I saw *Friday the 13th.* Whenever the girl went into the water and Jason stuck a knife in her and all this blood was in the water — I got real scared." (9,p.28)

Abelman and Sparks indicated that:

As the child moves into the eight- to twelve-year age range and begins to appreciate the difference between reality and fantasy, physical violence becomes particularly threatening. The child in this age range is capable of realizing that these depictions are completely possible. At the same time, they have little practice in coping with the harsh realities implied by such graphic violence." (9,p.28)

Children today have an easy access to frightening and violent programs available to their homes through movie channels. Fear can be handled by implementing five-fold family policy. First, maintaining a warm and serene family atmosphere. Second, helping the child with the selections of programs to watch. Third, explaining why violence is used in television programs. Fourth, encouraging the child to talk about stressful and fearful situations they experienced on television. Fifth, setting up adult models of critical viewing of television a child can imitate.

# REFERENCES

1. Dale, Edgar. *The Content of Motion Pictures,* New York: The Macmillan Company, 1935.

2. Schramm, Wilbur, et. al., *Television in the Lives of Our Children,* Stanford, California: Stanford University Press, 1961.

3. Singer, Robert, "Children, Aggression & Television," *Television & Children,* Fall 1982. pp.57-63.

4. Gross, Larry, "Television & Violence," in *Television Awareness Training, The Viewer's Guide for Family & Community,* Ben Logan (Ed.) Abingdon/Nashville, 1979. (pp.19-23)

5. Siegel, Alberta, "Learning and TV Violence," in *Television Awareness Training, The Viewer's Guide for Family & Community,* Ben Logan (Ed.) Abingdon/Nashville, 1979. (pp. 231-237).

6. Hefzallah, I. and Rex Page. "An Examination of TV Violence," unpublished paper, Fairfield University, Summer 1985.

7. "White-Collar Crime: Booming Again," *The New York Times,* Sunday, 6/09/85.

8. Cross, Donna Woolfolk, *Mediaspeak, How TV Makes Up Your Mind,* A Mentor Book, 1984.

9. Abelman, Robert & Glen G. Sparks. "Can TV Really Frighten Children?" *Television & Families,* Winter 1985. pp. 27-30.

# Chapter  X

## SEX ON TELEVISION

*Television's messages about sex are hidden, inaccurate, comic, and violent. Until television changes its portrayal of sex, it is extremely essential to develop young people's understanding of proper human sexuality and the difference between that and the televised portrayal of sex.*

### Relative Lack of Concern about Sex on Television

More attention has been given by the public to the amount of television violence and its possible harmful effects than to sex on television and how it can shape young people's attitude toward human sexuality. For instance, the majority of the respondents to a survey conducted by Joyce Sprafkin, et al believed TV violence to be more of a problem than TV sex. Ninety-one percent agreed that there is too much violence on television while only 63% agreed that there is too much sex on television. Further, when asked, "Which is more harmful for children to see on TV?", violence was noted by 48% and sex by only 3%; nevertheless, 44% responded that both are equally bad. (1,p.313)

The researchers hypothesized that:

the predominance of violence over sex as a concern may relate to the geographic area in which the study was conducted. It is possible that the people in this area (Long Island) are generally more liberal about sex and more concerned about violence than a similar sample of people from the south or midwest would be. In light of this, the fact that more than half the sample considered sex as unsuitable for viewing by children cannot be overlooked. (1,p.313)

During the time of the study, it was noted that on TV there was:

an increase in the frequency of certain kinds of sexual portrayals, specifically flirtatious behavior, suggestive comments, and contextually implied intercourse. On the other hand, what has remained consistent over the years (76-78) is that explicit behaviors (such as intercourse) are never actually seen on the screen, but are only

95

referred to verbally or contextually implied, and that a large portion of the references to sexuality occur in a humorous format. (1,p.304)

Such is not the case today. Pay television channels have brought to home viewers explicit portrayal of sexual acts including intercourse. For instance, *Risky Business* played the summer of '85 on movie channels presented the story of a teen-ager teaming up with prostitutes to sell sexual pleasure to other teen-agers. He made a tremendous profit in one night, enough to restore his father's Porsche which was accidently driven into Lake Michigan, and to buy back his parents' furnishings from the previous pimp. In that movie, two incidents of explicit intercourse between the boy and the prostitute were portrayed.

Lack of overall concern about sex on television, as compared to that of violence on television, is due to many factors.

1. "Concerns about television sex are clearly related to individual differences which determine sensitivity to the issue." (1,p.304) With the sexual freedom which came upon us in the sixties, breaking many taboos, parents might be lenient toward sex as portrayed on television.

2. There is an underlying belief that entertainment and recreation are harmless, and since sex on television is used primarily to evoke fun and laughter, there is no harm done. In a Sprafkin study, a majority of 65% disagreed with a linkage between teen-age promiscuity and televised sex; and 55% believed televised sexual innuendoes to be harmless. (1,p.313)

3. Some parents find it difficult to talk with their children about sex. TV does. Hopefully, they think that their children will learn something about sex from television. In the Sprafkin et al study, 45% of the parents responding to the inquiry "...felt that seeing new sex information might cause children to 'initiate useful discussions with their parents,' and 19 percent felt children might 'learn something positive.' Further, 73 percent of the adults indicated that at some time, sexual content on TV had prompted a discussion in their households, and that the ensuing discussion was a positive or useful experience for 51 percent of these and a negative one for only 5 percent." (1,p.313)

4. There is a consistency between messages the total culture gives to adolescents about sexuality and sexuality on TV. Highlights of these messages are:
   — Nice girls don't plan; real boys score;
   — Sex is secretive and dangerous, and not to be discussed seriously;
   — Worthwhile women don't pursue sexual expression; i.e., bad girls do it for fun, while good girls do it for love (note that a

majority of parents still approve of premarital sex for boys and disapprove of it for girls);
— Real men's sexual feelings are so strong that they are uncontrollable, and may even be expressed with violence;
— Sex is something wrested from women, not something that is shared with them;
— All affection or touching must culminate in sex;
— Sex is a matter of techniques, not feelings or experiences. (2,p.20)

Exploiting such myths is dangerous. If the society without being critical adopted certain attitudes, some of which are illogical, such as the double standard expressed in the above list (first and third points), it becomes imperative to mass media to correct wrong messages in an attempt toward improving the quality of life. In addition, the medium cannot ignore sincere criticism by caring parents, educators, social and religious leaders.

Statistics of teen-age sexuality (1.3 million teen pregnancies in the U.S. in 1982) are frightening. (2,p.19) It is wrong to solely blame television for teen-age promiscuity. However, what does television do to cure the situation? The unfortunate answer is that it reinforces a tragic situation.

5. Some adults find vicarious sexual experience in watching television sex. A large percentage of viewers of sex channels on television and X-rated movies are not teen-agers, but adults. Accordingly, those adults are in no position to enforce decent material on television.

6. Parents are caught in the trap of sexual revolution. No longer are standard and sex-gratifying values clearly defined and adhered to. To say "no" to sexual behavior which was considered years back as improper might label parents as traditional and not up-to-date with the new way of life.

## HOW DOES TV PORTRAY SEX?

### *Sex on Pay Channels*

It should be noted at the outset of this discussion that there is a marked difference between open broadcast channels and pay television channels in portrayal of sex. There is not a day of the week that a pay television channel does not carry an R-rated program. In the brief description of the program in the cable guide, reasons for labelling the program as an R program are usually listed, such as nudity, violence, adult theme, etc.

In open broadcast, sexual intercourse is either contextually implied, or referred to. In pay television channels, sexual intercourse is explicitly presented, and in many instances, just for the sake of showing a naked couple in passion.

As was mentioned earlier in the book, TV is a hungry medium for talent. To satisfy long hours of broadcast on a large number of channels, and to compete for an audience, TV program makers unfortunately look for a fast production filled with cheap thrills. There is nothing that can be more easily and cheaply produced than sex scenes.

As a result of cheap techniques of attracting an audience, pay television channels are full of uncalled for sex scenes adding to the confusion of uncertain teen-agers as to what love is.

## Sex on Open-Broadcast Channels

Flirting behavior, innuendoes, and references to sex have been on the increase. For instance, flirting behavior quadrupled in frequency from 1975-1977 from less than one per hour to three per hour. Innuendoes also increased in the same period from one to about seven per hour. (3,p.88) From 1977 to present, there are reasons to believe that sexual content is on the increase. Leading soap operas and some prime-time shows such as *Dynasty* are saturated with scenes of infidelity, flirtations, and innuendoes.

Popular shows among children and teen-agers such as *Happy Days* presented Fonzie as a teen-age hero who can score with any girl he desires at the snap of his fingers. *Three's Company* portrays two beautiful young women sharing an apartment with a young man. Their upstairs bachelor neighbor is a used-car salesman whose main interest in every show is the women he dates. In the early shows, the Ropers, a middle-aged couple, resided in a downstairs apartment. Mr. Roper was the building manager. Mrs. Roper was portrayed as a sexually frustrated wife. The new show replaced the Ropers with a strangely, decoratively dressed, and not-so-smart Mr. Farley. Both Mr. Roper and Mr. Farley suspect Jack to be a homosexual. Facial expressions, gestures, and dialogue in that show are loaded with sex hidden in a humorous context.

## TV MESSAGES ABOUT SEX

### 1. Hidden Messages

TV messages about sex are indirect. They are hidden or implied, and are often communicated in innuendoes or suggestive visuals. Sex on television is an acceptable subject if it is humorous. Canned laughter, or a cheerful reaction of the studio audience emphasize the implied sex messages.

Sex is also acceptable on television if it is presented as a crime. Very often rape is presented as a crime of passion, contrary to the fact that it is a violation of the rights and freedom of another individual.

2. *Inaccurate Messages*

   (a) Sex on television is rarely presented in the context of real relation-ships. It is seldom to show the inner conflict that people might have about free sex. Teen-agers' confusion about sex is rarely seen. There is a great deal of casual sex without any emotional attachment or consequences (no wonder there are so many unwanted pregnancies among sexually active teen-agers).

   (b) Adults practice free sex as fun and a fast game. A TV hero is usually single, and in almost every episode, the hero can have a new romance. It is common for 007 movies to end the film with James Bond in an intimate scene with a new romance.

   Usually the hero is surrounded with extremely attractive women dressed to sexually attract not only the actors in the story, but also the audience, who experiences an enactment of their sexual and adventurous fantasies.

   (c) Unfortunately, sex is presented as an equal to love, or as a test of love. One of the television male cliches is asking the female for sex as a proof of her love.

   (d) In our television culture, a man and a woman's encounter has to end in the bedroom. What a way of reducing human relationship into one aspect of human sexuality. Rather than portraying males and females as equal partners in a relationship, TV perpetuates the notion of men and women as opposites, and sex as being the only aspect of that relationship.

   (e) On television, men are stereotypically ambitious, competitive, smart, dominant, and at times, violent. They think logically and are seldom beset by strong emotions.

   On the other hand, women on television tend to be sensitive, romantic, warm, submissive, timid, and very attractive. They are often over-emotional and unable to solve their problems without depending on a male character.

   Men are interested in women for erotic reasons. Sexual activity then becomes a matter of male performance with emphasis on how good the male was in bed. Success or failure in the sexual act overshadows love, concern, and friendship, and thus puts young people under a great deal of pressure. Females are constantly reminded of the need to be attractive and the males are constantly

99

reminded of manhood as being capable of scoring and being a skilled sexual performer.

One of the most prevalent themes which recurs on television is portraying sex as a manipulative technique through which people, especially women, achieve power.

(f) Marriage on television is not that glamorous. Girls can be sexually attractive to boys, but when the question of marriage arises, abandoning the relationship becomes the male's solution to the problem. Male's love and tenderness are seldom shown. Males are supposed to be macho men who never cry. Heroes of adventure stories are usually singles allowing the producer the ease of engaging the hero in a sexual adventure and romance without working out a family commitment in the story.

Married men on television are boring, and marriage itself could be dull. Infidelity is common among married couples on TV. There are few programs like *The Bill Cosby Show* in which the audience can see married couples' romanticism, or a family life that can be fun. Accordingly, teen-agers have few characters they can look up to. Role-modeling becomes a problem with television's repeated attempts to portray sex trivially.

In general, sex is inaccurately and trivially presented on television with the emphasis on the sensual rather than on presenting lasting and committed relationships between the male and female. With lack of sex education in schools, and lack of family discussions on human sexuality, young people tune in to find answers in television programs. Unfortunately, the answers are inaccurate, misleading, and emphasize a human sexuality myth that should be challenged and not exploited.

Television has to look closely at its current practice of cheap, comic, and violent portrayal of sex. Casual presentations of sensitive issues should be avoided. Life is not all sex, nor is sex the answer to personal and social problems. Sanitizing sex by concealing its consequences does not help young people in making wise decisions in their sexual lives.

Until TV changes its portrayal of sex, it is extremely essential to develop young people's understanding of proper human sexuality and the difference between that and the televised portrayal of sex. Teens need to develop appreciation of personal values, resistance to peer pressure, and an ability to examine television values.

# REFERENCES

1. Sprafkin, Joyce N., Theresa L. Silverman, and Eli A. Rubinstein, "Reactions to Sex on Television: An Exploratory Study" in *Public Opinion Quarterly,* 1980, 00.303-315.

2. Klein, Marty, "Teens, Sexuality, and Prime Time Entertainment," *Television & Children,* Summer 1983, pp.19-25.

3. Franzblau, Susan, "Sexuality on the Screen," in *Television Awareness Training, The Viewers Guide for Family & Community,* Ben Logan (Ed.), Abingdon/Nashville, 1979, pp. 87-90.

# Chapter XI

# TV COMMERCIALS

*Selling a product by advertising it in a thirty-second TV interval to a noncaptive audience forms the big challenge for TV advertising. The commercial has to be attractive, interesting, informative, persuasive, and entertaining.*

*Commercials appeal to the basic needs and wants of the prospective viewer and rarely appeal to the logical and intellectual aspects of the viewer's personality. A commercial's prime intention is to impress and persuade the viewer. In their attempt to persuade, commercials could have undesirable effects on the viewers, especially young people who lack the experience to differentiate between the television commercial world and real life.*

## INTRODUCTION

Commercial television is in the business of selling the presence of an audience to the advertiser. (1) Entertaining programs as well as informational programs such as television news and special reports are structured to allow for commercial breaks. Usually, the program is structured to motivate the viewer to stay tuned in to follow the continuation of an exciting event interrupted by the commercial break.

People's behavior during the commercial break differs from one person to the other, and from one situation to another. Sometimes we just stay waiting for the program to resume. Other times, commercials give us a break to invade the kitchen for a fast snack, to go to the bathroom, to glance at a newspaper, or to talk briefly with other family members watching the program with us. There is not one specific pattern of behavior that an individual follows every commercial break. One thing for sure, we invariably watch commercials and in many instances we are affected by them even if we claim that we are not.

Business is an intelligent and efficient institution. Cost effectiveness of any venture is carefully calculated. If there is no evidence that businesses are reaching and affecting their potential clients, then spending millions of dollars every year on television advertising is unjustifiable. The profile of money spent in television advertising is a solid indication that advertising on television works. TV commercial expenditures increased from 300 million dollars in 1952 (1,p.43) to around 16 billion dollars in 1983. (2) Advertising is essential to a healthy economy. Through advertising, consumers are made aware of new products, specific values and advantages of other products and services. However, television commercials go beyond informing the audience. They aim at persuading the viewer to buy the advertised product. In many instances, the average viewer is not aware of the persuading elements of the commercials. Accordingly, his / her defense mechanism against being persuaded is not activated and the commercial has a better chance of achieving its intended effect.

Relatively few people accept the above claim. The majority of the audience believes that they are not affected by advertising and that they really make up their own minds. In their view, advertising in television is irrelevant, stupid, below their intelligence, foolish, and ineffectual. These are the people that are sold the fastest. They are the largest consumers without knowing why. As Wilson Bryan Key suggested:

> Like it or not, each one of us is continuously and strongly affected by advertising . . . If there is a significant difference between North Americans' response to media, it is a problem of how much they respond, not of whether or not they do. (3,p.80)

It is incredible that assertions of not believing or not being influenced by a commercial is exactly what advertising intends to happen; as Key put it, "...a very necessary illusion media must perpetuate in order to succeed in making up their minds for them." (3,p.79) He also said, " . . . they (audience) react to television commercials with a feeling of superiority that permits them to believe they are in control . . . People are prone to trust anything over which they believe they have control." (3,p.158)

Marshall McLuhan emphasized the same idea by referring to "the voice of the literate man, floundering in a milieu of ads, (who) boasts, 'Personally, I pay no attention to ads.'" (4,p.32)

Surrounded by a wealth of ads in print, graphic, and electronic media, it is impossible not to pay attention, especially when these ads are designed to reach the unconscious or subconscious mind. A mature graduate student who was working on a content analysis of dairy products television commercials reported,

> I found after viewing the commercials for this project that I wanted to buy dairy products in the worst way. I don't think at one time I ever had so much ice cream, yoghurt, and cottage cheese in my possession! Even though my intent was to see what made a person

buy and therefore be more aware, I was sold! Those sneaky, pesky, 'residual impressions' had me quite naturally buying more dairy products than I could use. It was, and is, a fascinating phenomenon to me. (5)

According to Vance Packard (6,p.127), advertisers seek to instill "residual impressions" on one's consciousness. The "residual impressions" that the researcher was referring to in the dairy products sample she analyzed were images emphasizing the freshness, smoothness, and richness of the product and the oral pleasure of consuming the product. In her words:

> The packaging of the ice cream showed condensation on the outside to emphasize freshness, the fruit ingredients were perfectly shaped and brightly colored, . . . there was always a stirring, swirling, or scooping motion sometimes done in slow motion to emphasize richness and smoothness of the ice cream . . . the mouth, tongue and lips played an exaggerated role in eating . . . the mouth must be wide open to encompass the vast amount being put in it. Ingenuity of the tongue and lips must be shown in conquering the overwhelming portion. Very sensual and seductive licking, smacking, and chewing motions were evident, showing voluptuousness and oral indulgence. (5)

TV commercials are skillfully structured to persuade the audience to buy a product. They stimulate and create a mass market by creating the need for the viewer to buy a product, even if that need does not really exist.

Motivating and persuading non-captive viewers to buy a product has to be done in the span of thirty seconds. The commercial, therefore, has to be attractive, interesting, informative, persuasive, and entertaining. Accordingly, as Peter Drucker put it, "Few messages are as carefully designed and as clearly communicated as the thirty-second commercial." (7) In every second, both audio and visual content have to be "precision engineered to accomplish a specific end — sell the product." (3,p.158)

Commercials primarily appeal to the basic needs and wants of the prospective viewer and rarely appeal to the logical and intellectual aspects of the viewer's personality. (8,p.81) A commercial's prime intention is to *impress* the viewer with the product and leave with him/her a vivid visualization of it. The verbal stimuli are carefully chosen and arranged to elicit the intended response. The images are composed and edited to visually communicate and persuade the viewer. Every element in the commercial, and how it is presented, is done for specific reasons. In four content analysis studies of television commercials (Hefzallah, et al 5,9,10,11), it was demonstrated that the choice of locale, major and supporting characters, type of action, the visual composition of the shots, the sound track including the verbal language, sound effects, and music were carefully done and efficiently used to maximize the effectiveness of the commercial. Whatever is said visually or orally in a commercial must be stated quickly and memorably. (12,p.106) The test for an effective commercial, as Otto Kleppner indicated, is not having the viewer say, "That's a good commercial," but rather, "That's a good product." (13,p.428) The product has to be appreciated and remembered despite the fact that it was presented in the midst of a flood of television commercials, each one selling its product with the same degree of urgency.

To meet this challenge, the advertiser prepares his material, as Wainright put it, "to overpower his competition." (12,p.106) To gain attention, the commercial maker might do something out of the ordinary (14,p.265), yet construct his commercial to make the viewer correctly remember and identify the product.

Attracting the viewer's attention is the beginning of selling a product. Holding the viewer's attention is a prerequisite to communicating the commercial's message. TV viewers form a noncaptive audience. The commercial break, moreover, has its inherent problems. Significant among these problems are:

(1) the tendency among some viewers to use the commercial break for carrying on other activities, such as talking to family members, eating, or reading the newspaper;

(2) that the commercial break sometimes presents an undesired break in the flow of either information or entertaining programs, which might irritate viewers.

To hold the attention of viewers under these circumstances, the commercial has to be worth watching. To achieve this objective, advertisers apply two major approaches:

(1) presenting what the viewer can believe is useful;

(2) developing the commercial into a miniprogram.

All of this has to be done in a well-defined design or a structure.

Book and Cary reported that

... in a continuing research study for an important TV advertiser .. . commercials with strong, well-defined structure registered much more effectively than those in which there was little or no design. Not only were the better-structured commercials better remembered, there was evidence that they were also superior in influencing the decision to buy." (15,p.7)

Different approaches may be applied to studying the structure of commercials. On the basis of an empirical analysis of TV commercials, six major types of TV-commercial structural design were defined. (16) Before explaining these types, we will review some attempts to classify and define the structure of TV commercials and the limitations of these classifications.

## TV COMMERCIALS' STRUCTURE

Book and Cary indicated the following types of structure of commercials: (15)

(1) *story line:* telling a story that involves tension at the outset and leads to a logical conclusion.

(2) *problem-solution:* based on a predicament or problem, then enlightenment, and, consequently, happy results with aid of the product.

(3) *chronology:* delivering the message through a series of related scenes, each scene progressing from the one before. It is an orderly, progressive, logical development, and it leads the viewer step by step to the concluding sell.

(4) *special effects:* striving for a mood that relates to the product and its uses.

(5) *testimonial:* matching the product with a believable celebrity, competent to pass judgment on such a product.

(6) *satire:* generally considered to be sophisticated wit that points up human foibles. As used in TV commercials, satire is written to be produced in an exaggerated style. Overdone wit can easily turn into heavy-handed slapstick.

(7) *spokesman:* similar to a radio commercial, but illustrated by a moving picture of the product and the announcer.

(8) *demonstration:* proving the product's superiority by showing the audience that the product does what it claims to do.

(9) *suspense:* begins with suspense, builds it carefully, then ends it with clarity and relevance.

(10) *slice-of-life:* slice-of-life structure is not essentially unlike the problem-solution. The difference is most often one of degree and use of technique.

(11) *analogy:* the "just as, so too" approach — using one example to explain another by comparison or implication.

(12) *fantasy:* relating fantasy to the product without obscuring the selling idea — e.g., the Green Giant.

107

(13) ***personality:*** a technical variant of the spokesman or announcer-on-camera straight-sell structure. It relies on an actor or actress rather than an announcer to deliver the message. It uses a setting rather than the background of a studio.

Close examination of the above indicates an overlap among story-line, problem-solving, slice-of-life, and suspense structures. In these four cases the need to buy the product is demonstrated by means of a plot in which a problem is first presented and then solved by the use of the product. An overlap also exists between the chronology and spokesman structures, since both present information orally, accompanied by appropriate visuals. The format is similar to an illustrated lecture. An overlap also appears between the testimonial and personality structures, since both apply a very similar approach. Moreover, analysts may identify a commercial's structure according to a dominant element in the audio and visual clues of the commercial, such as special effects, or distinguish its structure on the basis of technical variance.

In *Writing for TV and Radio*, Hilliard (8) indicated six commercial formats:

(1) ***straight sell:*** a direct statement about the product.

(2) ***testimonial:*** a testimonial given by a celebrity whose social and economic status is likely to be higher than that of the average viewer.

(3) ***humor:*** stressing mood and feeling, and possibly varying from gentleness to outright satire — e.g., Alka-Seltzer: "I can't believe I ate the whole thing."

(4) ***music:*** the message is sung and / or accompanied by a music score.

(5) ***dramatization:*** a short play creating suspense and reaching a climax, which is the revelation of the attributes of the product.

(6) ***other formats:*** two effective appeals involve family and children. The viewer identifies strongly and is left with a good feeling toward the product.

Close examination of Hilliard's commercial formats reveals an agreement with Book and Cary on two types — the testimonial and dramatization formats. It also shows that some formats can be identified by the dominant communication element in the commercial, such as the music and humor formats.

In Nelson's interesting book *The Design of Advertising*, the author discusses seven categories of TV commercials: (14)

(1) ***story:*** the introduction of a problem and its solution by the use of the product.

(2) **slice-of-life:** creating the impression that the commercial is a piece of nonfiction.

(3) **testimonial:** famous people or unknowns tell what they like about a product and urge, directly or indirectly, others to try it.

(4) **announcer:** a more direct selling approach, showing an announcer who tells the viewers why they should try a product.

(5) **demonstration:** showing how the product works and what it looks like.

(6) **song and dance:** employing the gaiety and flavor of a musical extravaganza.

(7) **special effects:** employing camera tricks, optical and electronic effects.

Nelson's system of classification is similar to Book and Cary's in some respects and similar to Hilliard's in others. Nelson and Book and Cary agree on six categories: slice-of-life, testimonial, announcer (spokesman), demonstration, and special effects. Nelson agrees with Hilliard on four categories: story (dramatization), testimonial, announcer (straight sell), and song and dance (music).

Close examination of Nelson's categories reveals an overlapping among the categories, and name a category by the dominant element in the commercials, such as song and dance. Overlapping structure categories and naming a structure by a dominant audio or visual element or by a technique of presentation are common among the previous studies.

Discussing the idea of "mutually exclusive classification," Book and Cary (15) explained: "Most of the structures are not mutually exclusive. A personality structure and a story line can be superimposed and used effectively. One, however, dominates: the secondary one can be considered as a technique on close scrutiny." (15,p.8)

I believe, first, that it is necessary to draw a distinction between the structure of the commercial and the techniques employed. Advertisers can present a story-line structure employing animation techniques or live action or live action and animation. They can also present a commercial in a modern setting or in a setting of earlier times. The structure will always be the same — a story line. Only the techniques will be different.

Second, it is possible to present distinct categorical structures of TV commercials. In a comprehensive content analysis of television commercials, Hefzallah and Maloney identified six distinct structural designs or plans: (17)

(1) **association:** the commercial associates the product with pleasant experiences, either past or present.

(2) ***demonstration:*** the commercial demonstrates the product to show how it looks and how it functions.

(3) ***informative:*** the commercial presents information on the product to impress the viewer with the quality of the product.

(4) ***plot:*** the commercial presents a problem which is answered by using the product.

(5) ***staged:*** the commercial stages an action where the product is used and the people using it are satisfied with it.

(6) ***testimonial:*** a famous person praises the product.

The above six plans do not overlap. It is possible to apply more than one plan in designing a commercial, such as combining the informative plan with the testimonial plan. But to achieve simplicity of message in a clear-cut form, an integrated plan within a thirty-second commercial might tend to complicate the message and/or its right presentation. To further illustrate these plans, an analysis of six commercials taken from the Clio Award Winners of 1973 follows. (17)

(1) *The Association Plan* (Example — Coca-Cola, "Country Sunshine;" Agency and Producer: McCann Erickson/Horn-Griner). A young woman goes back home to the country to visit her folks. She is dressed in modern clothing, but the taxicab looks thirty years old, emphasizing the simple life that those good people lead. The taxi driver is an old man; the road is dusty. The great-grandfather is still living, kids are playing together, and various animals are about. The girl is coming from the city "where life is more exciting." Yet she was "raised on country sunshine," and feels happy with "simple things." She has left her lover, saying to him, "I love you, please believe me. I wouldn't want you to ever leave me. But I was raised on country sunshine," and she has returned to the simple things like Coca-Cola and country sunshine.

From this analysis we observe that the product is orally associated with "country sunshine" and visually associated with simple, loving, and healthy surroundings. The appeal in the commercial is emotional. Wainright has observed that soft-drink commercials "have their primary appeal to young people. They show happy, healthy boys and girls having fun. There is a bright, catchy music track (and jingle) pulsating to the action. Although the commercial formula might change from year-to-year, the basic style is the same. Smart, handsome people who are on the go." (12,pp.272-3)

(2) *The Demonstration Plan* (Example — Mercedes Benz, "Ballet;" Agency and Producer: Ogilvy & Mather/Sentinel). The product is presented in its top performance as "Six Mercedes Benz test drivers perform a high-

speed ballet in the new 250SL." In this performance the narrator invites/ leads/tells us to pay particular attention to the following: "A car so responsive that six can react as one." As we listen to the narration, we watch a daring ballet performance. Sound effects emphasize the point of high-speed driving, and use of long focal-length lenses decreases the apparent distance between cars. Thus the ballet performance looks more daring, and we are amazed at the degree of responsiveness that the six cars demonstrate in this high-speed driving.

"New design." As we watch the performance the narrator says, "A car so incredibly designed, it took five years to develop." Today, when the common man knows that a lot goes into research to improve products, the fact that it took five years to develop this new car means that the car is trouble free and can give a great performance, as demonstrated on the screen.

This statement is followed by a more technical statement on improvements in rear suspension and in the engine. The word "new" precedes the items that have been improved. The statement reads: "With a *new* rear suspension, a *new* overhead cam, fuel-injected V-8 engine." The narrator proceeds to say, "Totally *new* body design, disc brakes on all four wheels." As we get to the last statement we see a head-on shot apparently taken with a long-focal-length lens — the picture looks flat. A road marker is seen in the way of the car line. The distance looks very short between the first car in the row and the obstacle. We are conditioned to the fact that the cars are running at a very high speed. We ask ourselves: Will the car be able to stop before hitting the obstacle? Suddenly, to raise the level of suspense, a car pulls out from behind the first car, takes over, and moves ahead of the first car. Then it stops before hitting the obstacle. As we see this brake performance we hear the narrator saying "disc brakes on all four wheels."

In this example the commercial presents the product by itself at its top performance level. In other instances, the product might be compared to another leading competitor to visually demonstrate its superiority. In either approach, the alleged qualities of the product are usually demonstrated visually and reinforced orally.

(3) *The Informative Plan* (Example — Del Monte, "Salmon:" Agency and Producer: McCann Erickson/MacGillivary-Foreman). A salmon is swimming upstream and along the diagonal of the frame in slow motion. There are realistic sound effects, deep-water sounds, accompanying the narrator as he says, "A Del Monte salmon contains no preservatives, no artificial food coloring. It does contain vitamin A (and) niacin . . . Pound for pound it contains as much protein as a raw T-bone steak. The more you know about salmon, the better for Del Monte." The next sequence is a series

111

of 44 stills of Del Monte canned products, each one being projected for about 1/12 second, followed by a Del Monte canned salmon which is projected for 5/12 second before it fades out. Fast country-style music accompanies the sequence. Although the average viewer cannot identify the other 44 products, he can get the impression that the company emphasizes quality and that it has a wide variety of products.

In this example the quality of the product is described using technical, yet familiar, food terms — ie., "no preservatives," "no artificial flavor," "no food coloring," "vitamin A," "niacin," "protein." These terms make up 28 percent of the narration. Excluding the producer's slogan, these terms make up 38 percent of the words used in the product's information.

Advertisers usually present information on the product in this plan orally and visually. They emphasize quality without attempting to substantiate the alleged information other than presenting a sample of the product.

(4) *The Plot Plan* (Example — Yamaha Motorcycles, "Birthday"; Agency and Producer: Botsford Ketchum/N. Lee Lacy). A middle-aged woman is celebrating her birthday. Her family (husband and two sons) guides her blindfolded through the back yard, where we see laundry on the clothesline, to the garage. Her surprise birthday present is a Yamaha. The lady is portrayed as a short, fat, unathletic housewife whose main job is housework. For this lady, owning a Yamaha, a symbol of sportsmanship and young athletic people, is a surprise. But the real surprise is when she discovers how easy it is to handle the motorcycle and how much fun it is to ride. As she sits on the seat of her new motorcycle listening to her husband explaining to her how to operate it, we see her holding a plate with a big portion of birthday cake. This shot emphasizes the pre-established concepts:

(1)  overweight, middle-aged housewife;
(2)  how easy it is to operate this machine, since the housewife can get all the instruction she needs while eating a piece of cake.

The next logical thing is to see her riding in the company of her husband and two sons. To help distinguish her from the others, since she is the center of the action, the producer has given her a yellow helmet to wear while her sons and husband wear basic white helmets. To further emphasize the surprise element, we see an old lady, probably one of the neighbors, looking startled as she watches the parade of motorcycles.

To emphasize how much fun it is to ride a Yamaha, the producer applied three things. First, the music was very effective — it was light and happy. Second, all of the major characters had big smiles on their faces. Third, the last shot, we see the parade approaching the driveway, the housewife at the rear of the line. As the husband and his sons drive into the driveway we expect to see the lady following. But to our surprise, she bypasses the driveway and continues her ride. How much fun it is! "Someday you'll own a Yamaha" regardless of your age or occupation. We get this message through two channels: First, we hear it, and then we see it written on the screen.

The theme is simple. It is fun to own and easy to use the product; therefore, if you are middle-aged, you can still enjoy life like young people. Commercials employing the plot plan establish a need for the product. We (Hefzallah & Maloney) noted a tendency in plot commercials to use half the time to present the problem and half the time to present the product as the solution to the problem. We (Hefzallah & Maloney) also noted a tendency to present realistic situations within which the need for the product is developed. (16)

The needs manifested in plot commercials are various, yet they are all centered around the security and comfort of the average viewer. Some of those needs are personal — clothing, hygiene, and self-identification; professional; emotional; financial; safety; political; family; transportation; pets; "nice time;" and relaxation.

(5) *The Staged Plan* (Example — Gillette Platinum Plus, "Father/Son:" Agency and Producer: J.W. Thompson/D. Richards). Producers present the product as having been used in the family for two generations because of its superiority. The music, the warm colors, the hair styles of the actors, and the old and the new bathroom designs, all set the stage for dear family memories — a child watching his father shaving. The message is that "Gillette is making a better double edge now than the one your father used . . . and someday Gillette will make even a better blade for your son." The superiority of the product is conveyed through the satisfaction and the smile of the fathers as they shave. Two still shots dissolve into one another, emphasizing the fact that the product has been around for a long time. In the first shot we see an old shaving mug, razor, and a pack of old Gillette blades. The sub-title on this shot reads "We made the first blade," and the narrator reads the same message. As the first shot dissolves into the next, we see the same shaving mug, razor, and a new pack of Gillette Platinum Plus. The sub-title reads "And we're still the first blade." Again, the narrator reads the same message.

In the staged plan people are shown using the product to achieve a certain goal. Satisfaction with the product is usually expressed orally through off-screen narration and visually through pantomime.

(6) *The Testimonial Plan* (Example — Datsun, "Dali/Wagon:" Agency and Producer: Parker/Cascade). Noted artist Salvador Dali was commissioned

to introduce the Datsun 610 five-door station wagon. The advertisers asked him to paint a portrait of this new car. His comment about the car is that it is "absolutely original, different, sensational." The abstract painting is used to introduce the car visually incorporating the ideas of originality, difference, and sensation. A ball in the center of the frame is moved upstage, gets smaller, then disappears. The car is now presented by fading it in the far horizon where the ball disappeared, then moving it downstage. As it moves downstage, it gets larger while items in the painting get smaller, until we see the car by itself.

Dali is then seen in a series of stills, inside and outside the car for about 10 seconds. Then, we see the car from the outside and the inside. The seats are animated, angles of view exaggerating the interior of the car in terms of space. The car looks roomy and beautiful. Dali opens the tailgate, picks up an easel and starts to leave. The car is moved upstage while the painting is moved downstage. A wipe is used; the whole shot gets smaller and occupies only two-thirds of the frame. So, in the last shot of the ad we see Dali, the car, the painting, and the written-verbal message "Datsun, from Nissan with pride."

In the testimonial plan, a celebrity whose socioeconomic status is usually upper-middle class (higher than that of the average viewer) gives a testimonial. The commercial implies that the product belongs to, or is used by, the celebrity. The words and the celebrity's action both emphasize the merit of the product.

## EFFECTS OF TV COMMERCIALS

In their attempt to persuade, commercials could have undesirable effects on the viewers, especially young people who lack the experience to differentiate between the TV commercials' world and real life.

TV commercials do not only sell products, they glamorously advocate a style of life in which:

1. one's worth is measured in terms of his/her possessions
2. one's worth is measured in terms of how one looks and smells
3. reality is mixed with fantasy — some products are shown to transform reality into fantasy
4. people's happiness is associated with material things
5. needs are created and satisfaction of those needs is met through possession and use of products
6. certain facts that will make the product more appealing are emphasized, and others are excluded
7. sex is exploited to attract and influence others — usually the use of the product is presented as a way to become more sexy and attractive

114

8. junk food is a treat
9. liquor, beer, and wine are presented as the best way to relax after a hard day of work or exercise
10. over-the-counter drugs are frequently presented as instant cures to ailments
11. there is an instant solution to problems one encounters in life.

Children are a more vulnerable audience who do not possess the skill to discriminate the style of life advocated by the commercials, nor the attractive claims about the product. Accordingly, some commercials could teach children misconceptions about life, create unrealistic expectations about what a product could do, and cause family conflict when a child is denied something he/she has seen on television.

Richard P. Adler, in a research study analyzing the effects of television advertising on children for the National Science Foundation, stated "It is clear from available evidence that TV advertising does influence children. Research has demonstrated that children attend to and learn from commercials." (18,p.ii).

Children's eyes and ears are constantly being deluged by televised drama, music video, comedy — and constantly being seduced by commercials. This seduction by advertisers is disturbing. Most child-directed advertising tends to create unrealistic and false images of people and society. Jerry Goodis, president of an ad agency in Toronto, commented, "The images your children are growing up with are not those of Washington, Jefferson, and Lincoln — they're images of Chevrolet, Colgate, and Coke ... they're images of commercials saying father is a jerk; mother is stupid and a gossip; all kids should make out; and elderly people sit around arthritic and constipated . . ." (19,p.200)

Fred Rogers, television's Mister Rogers, believes that "Commercialism bombards us all and all too frequently with messages which say you have to be something besides yourself to get along . . . Your resources are not enough, so be sure to buy ours. Our children are being raised on messages like this, and what is more, they think we adults condone them." (20, p.46) Lacking the experience to examine what they see and hear, children absorb the information presented to them through the commercial. Even adults, caught off-guard, will also absorb what the commercial is advocating.

Children need special protection until they develop critical viewing skills to examine television material carefully. That protection should come from responsible ad agencies, parents who take the time to discuss with their children their television experiences, schools which offer critical viewing curricula, and from responsible leaders in the society.

A step in the right direction has been taken by the development of *Children's Advertising Guidelines* (21) by the Children's Advertising Review Unit of the National Advertising Division. The Guidelines have been developed for the use of advertisers and advertising agencies and for self-regulation "to help ensure that advertising directed to children is truthful, accurate, and fair to children's perception." Five basic principles underline these guidelines:

(1) Advertisers should always take into account the level of knowledge, sophistication and maturity of the audience to which their message is primarily directed. Since younger children have a limited capability for evaluating the credibility of what they watch, they place a special responsibility upon advertisers to protect them from their own susceptibilities.

(2) Realizing that children are imaginative and that make-believe play constitutes an important part of the growing up process, advertisers should exercise care not to exploit that imaginative quality of children. Unreasonable expectations of product quality or performance should not be stimulated either directly or indirectly by advertising.

(3) Recognizing that advertising may play an important part in educating the child, information should be communicated in a truthful and accurate manner with full recognition by the advertiser that the child may learn practices from advertising which can affect his or her health and well-being.

(4) Advertisers are urged to capitalize on the potential of advertising to influence social behavior by developing advertising that, wherever possible, addresses itself to social standards generally regarded as positive and beneficial, such as friendship, kindness, honesty, justice, generosity and respect for others.

(5) Although many influences affect a child's personal and social development, it remains the prime responsibility of the parents to provide guidance for children. Advertisers should contribute to this parent-child relationship in a constructive manner. (21)

According to the Children's Advertising Reveiw Unit, "The Guidelines should not be regarded as prescribing rigid or inflexible rules which may deprive children and advertisers of the benefits of innovations and new approaches." The intent in all cases "should be to deal fairly and honestly with children fulfilling the spirit as well as the letter of the Guidelines." (21)

The Guidelines embrace advertising designed to appeal to children eleven years of age and under. They address the areas of commercials and social values, presentation techniques, endorsement of the product by characters, avoiding undue pressure to purchase, safety, and claim substantiation.

Self regulation of children's advertising by the advertising industry is not sufficient. The public has to monitor the implementation of the Guidelines. Some of the children's television commercials today are far from implementing "the spirit and the letter" of the Guidelines. This becomes more crucial if we consider the number of ads advertising similar products, such as cereals or toys, during children's viewing hours. For instance, in a 1982 study of food commercials broadcast on a Saturday morning from 6:00 a.m. to 12:00 p.m on one channel revealed that the majority of food commercials during that time were of highly sugared products, especially pre-sweetened cereals. (10)

In a more recent study (22), April 1985, analyzing children's commercials during a similar time-slot like the 1982 study, showed that during four telecast hours there were 70 food and toy commercials. Nutrition in food commercials was not emphasized, and only two toy commercials showed how the toys worked, while the rest attempted to entice the children by showing other children having a good time using them.

Advertising, especially for children, must be questioned and curtailed. Joseph Seldin pointed out, "Manipulation of children's minds in the fields of religions or politics would touch off a parental storm of protest and a rash of congressional investigations. But in the world of commerce, children are fair game and legitimate prey." (6,p.139)

---

Hand-in-hand with attempts to regulate children's advertising should be developing parents', children's, and young people's awareness of the persuasive intentions and techniques of television advertising — an objective that can be best achieved through critical viewing curricula in schools, and through parent-child discussions of television commercials.

# REFERENCES

1. Leibert, D.E., "Television Advertising and Values," in *Television Awareness Training, The Viewer's Guide for Family and Community,* B. Logan (Ed.) Abingdon/Nashville, 1979.

2. *Advertising Age,* 55:1, p.13, January 2, 1984

3. Key, Wilson Bryan, *Subliminal Seduction,* N.J.: A Signet Book, New American Library, 1974.

4. McLuhan, Marshall, *Understanding Media,* N.J.: A Mentor Book, New American Library, 1964.

5. Hefzallah, Ibrahim and Melanie Switz, "Content Analysis of Dairy Products Commercials," unpublished paper, Fairfield University, 1974.

6. Packard, Vance, *The Hidden Persuaders,* Peter H. Wyden, Inc., 1972.

7. Youngblood, Gene, *Expanded Cinema,* New York: E.P. Dutton and Co., 1970.

8. Hilliard, Robert, *Writing for TV and Radio,* 3rd Edition, New York: Hastings House, 1976.

9. Hefzallah, Ibrahim and W. Paul Maloney, "Content Analysis of TV Commercials," *International Journal of Instructional Media,* Vol. 5(1), 1977-78.

10. Hefzallah, Ibrahim and Donna Andrade, "Content Analysis of Jeans Commercials," unpublished research paper, Fairfield University, 1981.

11. Hefzallah, Ibrahim and Jean Emilia Hueg, "Content Analysis of TV Food Commercials," unpublished research paper, Fairfield University, 1982.

12. Wainright, Charles A., *Television Commercials: How to Create Successful TV Advertising,* New York: Hastings House, 1970.

13. Kleppner, Otto, *Advertising Procedure,* 6th Ed., Englewood Cliffs, N.J.: Prentice-Hall, 1974.

14. Nelson, Roy Paul, *The Design of Advertising,* 4th Ed., Dubuque: William Brown, 1981.

15. Book, Albert and Norman Cary, *The Television Commercial,* Chicago: Crain, 1970.

16. Hefzallah, Ibrahim and W. Paul Maloney, "Content Analysis of TV Commercials," *Monograph,* Fairfield University Library, 1975.

17. Hefzallah, Ibrahim and W. Paul Maloney, "Are There Only Six Kinds of TV Commercials?" *Journal of Advertising Research,* 1979, Vol 19, No. 4, pp. 57-62.

18. Adler, Richard P. et al, *Research on the Effects of Television's Advertising on Children,* Washington: Government Printing Office, 1970.

19. Little, Joseph Fletcher (Ed.), *Coping with Television,* Illinois: McDougal, Little and Co., 1974.

20. Sarson, Evelyn (Ed.), *Action for Children's Television,* New York: Avon Books, 1971.

21. Children's Advertising Review Unit, *An Eye on Children's Advertising Self-Regulation,* National Advertising Division, Council of Better Business Bureaus, N.Y., 1978.

22. Hefzallah, Ibrahim and Barbara Kindle, "Content Analysis of Children's TV Commercials," unpublished research paper, Fairfield University, 1985.

# Chapter XII

## TV NEWS

*Today, close to two-thirds of the population rely mainly on television for news. Surveys have shown that television is considered the most-believed medium. Advancement in video and telecommunications technology provides the viewers with the opportunity to witness events as they happen. Watching political and world leaders' reactions to national and world events has increased the credibility of the television medium in reporting immediate and relevant news.*

*Treated as a show, the producers design the news program, in the first place, to attract a large audience and keep it tuned in. Inherent in this practice are the shortcomings of television news.*

### *Definition*

The guiding principles for the news since the days of the American Revolution have been to "disseminate the news as quickly and accurately as possible to the largest number of people." (1p.171) Webster's New World Dictionary (2) defines the news as new information about anything, information previously unknown, recent happenings, and/or reports of such events. Accordingly, news is "factual and fresh." (3p.106) Unbiased and accurate news is imperative to the presentation of an objective, clear picture of the world in which we live.

To keep news and opinion separate has been a tradition respected by most publishers and editors. (1p.172)

The 1960s saw the beginning of a debate about advocacy journalism. Advocacy journalism is:

... the writing of stories with the deliberate intention of moving the reader to some social or economic action. This trend was initiated with the MUCKRAKERS in the early 20th century. Advocacy journalism has, however, principally been the province of the underground press, which flourished in the 1960s and early 1970s; writers for alternative political, religious, sexual, and life-style newspapers and magazines; and authors of best-selling books. (1p.172)

121

While network and local television news attempt to keep news unbiased, some special cable and satellite television channels are and will broadcast advocacy journalism.

Consumer-oriented news is also a new trend. With the wide selection of products and premiums available to the public, segments of news programs or special reports attempt to enlighten the consumer to make wiser decisions.

Human-oriented news is another trend in newscasting. Light stories focusing on people as humans, children, and pets are usually included in a thirty-minute news program. These stories, the weather, and the sports usually constitute the lighter side of the news program. The serious side focuses on crises, disasters, conflicts, political and social issues.

## *Development of TV News*

In the early days of television, TV news was tailored in a similar fashion like radio news. News items were read to the TV camera by a newscaster. The use of the visual dimensions of television was minimum.

As television became more common in households, TV news became more respectable. News documentary by news professionals such as Edward R. Murrow gave television news reporting credibility and well-thought of news programs. News reporters from newspapers were hired and sent out with camera crews to develop news stories utilizing both the audio and visual elements of the television medium. (3,p.103)

In the 1960s the spontaneity of live coverage of major events made television news more appealing to watch. Immediacy of news telecasting of important events as they were happening gave the public an awareness of a value that television has over newspapers and magazines. Seeing key people in the midst of events that were shaping the world gave the audience a sense of participation in those events. Over ninety-million people watched the historical debate between presidential candidates Richard Nixon and John Kennedy. The blanket coverage of President John F. Kennedy's assassination on November 22, 1963 forced the news department to stay on the air to keep the nation informed. According to Walter Lister, "Those four days of blanket coverage mark the time that network news came of age."(3) He further points out that "Coincidentally there was a major turning point for TV news in 1963. It was the first year, according to the Roper Organization, that people depended more on television than on newspapers to tell them what was going on in the world." (3p.103)

Today close to two-thirds of the population rely mainly on television for news. (3p.103) "Surveys have shown that television is considered the most believed medium." (1p.172) Advancement in video and telecommunications technology allowing on-location reporting regardless of the distance between the location and the stations gave the viewers the opportunity to travel vicariously to those locations to witness through the eyes of the reporter distant events as they are happening. Teleconferencing with key people and leaders from distant parts of the country and the world gave the opportunity to the public to listen and watch the reactions of political and world leaders to national and world events. These modern capabilities of the television medium increased its credibility in reporting immediate and relevant news.

The above advantages make television a powerful medium of communication. At the same time, they increase the responsibilities of news personnel toward the public. These responsibilities are best described in the following excerpt from the Television Code of the National Association of Broadcasters:

> . . . a television station's news schedule should be adequate and well-balanced. News reporting should be factual, fair and without bias . . . Good taste should prevail in the selection and handling of news. Morbid, sensational or alarming details not essential to the factual report, especially in connection with stories of crime or sex should be avoided. News should be telecast in such a manner as to avoid panic and unnecessary alarm.

A powerful medium of communication governed by well-stated ethics and manned by professional news staff should produce outstanding news service to the public, which it does in many instances, especially in special news coverage and reports. However, daily television news programs on networks and local stations in general have their limitations which a critical viewer should be aware of. These limitations are primarily due to treating the television news as a TV show that has to go on the air at a certain time.

## LIMITATIONS OF TV NEWS

Treated as a show, the producers design the news program, in the first place, to attract a large audience and keep it tuned in. Inherent in this practice are the shortcomings of television news.

### *Stories with Visual Appeal*

First, viewers are often denied information if it does not promise to be visually appealing to the general public, as Donna Cross put it, "Stories without a strong visual appeal . . . are rarely given more than cursory attention." (4p.62) Conklin reported the same in discussing characteristics of television news. He said, "Visual values are given priority over real news values, the question is often asked, 'Is this good footage?' (of film or tape)." (5p.99)

Cross gave an example of a good news story which was killed because of its potential lack of visualizations. She reported:

One former NBC producer proposed to do a story on Washington lobbyists, that enormously powerful group whose activities affect how the rest of us eat, drink, get paid, get taxed, have children, etc. But the story was killed before it even started. "We just couldn't show how lobbying goes on," says the producer. "Congress has rules that forbid filming in corridors, so we couldn't follow a lobbyist on his rounds. And although we could have used artists' renderings, it wouldn't have been very effective. (4p.63)

Lister underlined the same phenomenon. He said,

Putting news into an entertainment medium naturally invites show business techniques. Almost any story with good action pictures has a good chance of being broadcast, while a complicated economic report is hard to illustrate on television and has to be very important to rate more than passing mention. (3p.104)

Visualization of news items sometimes takes the route of sensationalism, and nothing is more sensational and easier to produce than violence, such as blood on the street after a crime has been committed, violent demonstrations, buildings on fire, etc.

Trivia that are visually appealing are considered as fun stories used to soften the effect of "bad news." "The longest hot dog in the city," "The most decorative tatoo," "The fastest man in peeling an apple," are possible samples of visualized trivia.

## Entertaining News Shows — Light in Information

Attempts are made to avoid producing news in the format of "talking heads" in which newscasters read the news to the camera. There is a common belief that there is nothing more boring than seeing a person talking all the time to the camera. However, one should not overlook the fact that if the topic is of importance, a simple presentation format does not lend the television experience boring. Millions of Americans tune in to watch talk shows, special news reports, presidential debates, news bulletins, etc. Because of the importance of the topic and people involved, a straight reading of the news with no visualization does not seem boring to the majority of the audience.

Unfortunately, television is viewed by television producers and the public in general as an entertainment medium. Therefore, to attract an audience to a news program, it has to be interesting and entertaining. The producers of news programs implement this principle and put entertainment as a criterion to be achieved in news programs. Accordingly, news programs are light in their information. With the exception of special news programs such as *60 Minutes,* news programs lack depth and breadth. When two-thirds of the population rely on television as their major source of news, the result is that Americans are not well-informed on important national matters.

As for understanding international issues, the situation is even worse. The average news viewer is not well-informed about the dynamics of the world's nations and the role of the U.S.A. as a leader of the free world. The covering of world news is very limited, especially on local stations.

As the world shrinks in space due to vast development in fast and efficient transportation and telecommunications means, Americans have to develop an understanding of world politics and economics. Yet, daily news shows focus on unrelated crises and disasters, which usually are presented on the average in less time than sports news. Apparently, a story's newsworthiness is often determined by distance. However, world events today are hitting home. The oil embargo of 1973, the Iranian crisis, trouble in Lebanon and in Latin America are no longer distant happenings. The public needs more than reporting on separate and unrelated events. It needs accurate and relevant information to understand the roots of those disturbances and crises. Light reporting and/or graphic presentation of these events are not enough. The question that networks have to help the viewer to answer is, "Why are all of these events happening?"

## A Half-Hour of Simplistic Presentations

A significant feature of today's world is the fast pace of widespread change in every phase of human lives. There are too many items worth reporting that occur every day. Accordingly, decisions on what to be presented in a news show is an on-going process. Some of the stories are considered as serious to report on. Others "should be used because they are fun, or poignant, or odd. They aren't important, but it is important to find them and make space for them. All the news doesn't have to be bad, or momentous." (6p.13)

National and international news, fun stories, sports, and weather have to be packed in a half-hour show, and because of the commercials, "they must be covered in twenty-two minutes. That's time for up to twenty stories, some of them covered in a few seconds, others in as much as five minutes." (6p.14) This simply does not give time for in-depth coverage especially when news stories are designed to capture and maintain the attention of viewers.

To capture the attention of viewers, first, a "hook," or a "lead" is used. In words of Chancellor and Mears, "Leads are the keynotes, the overtures, the tee shots of newswriting. Properly crafted, the lead answers questions before they are asked and promises more answers to follow. The lead sets the theme and points the way." (6,p.24)

To maintain the attentions of the viewers, the body of the news story features some kind of conflict. Usually, two opposite points of view are presented with no middle grounds, followed by concluding remarks by the newscaster.

As a result of the short time given each story, and the deliberate intention to capture and hold the attention of the viewers as described above, television news lacks in-depth coverage.

## Artificial Continuity of News Programs

To string twenty news stories in one show, producers look for transitions. Transitions take one of three forms.

The first can be described as artificial transition and it happens when the broadcaster leads into a story that has no connection with the one that ended. Capitalizing on a word in the closing statement, the announcer uses it in a sentence leading to the story to follow. Cross reported on an example of artificial transition. "One reporter was told by his producer to conclude a story about an alternate theory of creation with reference to bibles, even though the theory did *not* represent the biblical view and bibles had nothing to do with what the story was about. The reason? The following story began with a line about 'welfare cheaters swearing on a stack of bibles.' (4p.70)

The second type of transition is known as "Happy Talk." "Happy Talk" describes the brief, happy, short conversation that newscasters carry on among themselves. It commonly occurs before the weather, or the sports section of the program, and usually makes humorous reference to some sports event or the prediction of the weather.

The third type of transition is the "Teaser." The objective of the teaser is to attract the viewer to what is coming next on the news program.

Two types of teasers are commonly used. The first aims at enticing the viewer to tune in to watch the news show. Examples of this type of teasers are: "New drug to cure cancer. Details at eleven;" or "Twelve people dead. Cause is unknown. Details at six."

The second type of teaser aims at keeping the audience tuned in to resume watching the news program after a commercial break. For example, "Coming up next, traces of toxic material found in our drinking water,'" or, "Still ahead — heavy snow-storm predicted for tomorrow — when we continue."

Teasers underline the dramatic and exciting inclinations of television news. They also determine the sequencing of news items, not according to their importance, but according to their dramatic appeal.

## Heroes vs. Celebrities

To present interesting and varied personalities to the public, TV news programs introduce and keep the audience up-to-date on the news of their favorite celebrities and heroes. Juxtaposing news of celebrities to that of news can result in confusing heroes with celebrities.

A hero is a person who became famous for things he/she endured and achieved. A celebrity is a person well-known for his/her image or trademark. (4p.135)

In a survey reported by the *World Almanac,* based on a survey of about 4000 teenagers in 145 cities, Michael Jackson is the No. 1 hero of high school students. Eddie Murphy ranked second, followed by President Reagan. Actors Kevin Bacon and Clint Eastwood were the fourth and fifth, followed by basketball star Julius Erving, film stars Tom Cruise and Mr. T., rock artist Eddie Van Halen, and Katharine Hepburn. Of the ten heroes, only two — the President and Julius Erving — are not in show business. (7)

"The world still has heroes," says Cross, "but the glare of celebrity often casts them into the shadows." She explains:

The shift from hero- to celebrity-worship occurred around the turn of the century and was closely tied to the rise of new forms of media — first photography, and later moving pictures, radio, and television. These media gave fame in America an entirely new dimension — physical recognition . . . Slowly, the focus of public attention began to shift away from knowing what such people did to knowing what they looked like. (4p.135-136)

The world of young people needs models to look up to, a service that TV news departments can offer to young people. Celebrities gain expanded exposure through their work in the media. Heroes who endure and achieve are not well-known to young people.

## News on Time

News programs are prescheduled. The news copy and remote stories have to be ready in advance. Sometimes the pressure of meeting production and broadcast deadlines undermines the depth of the story. Simply, there is not much time to study the context of events. As a result, the coverage tends to be more of a headline and not a well-developed report. Lister pointed to the fact that, "If all the words spoken on a half-hour network news broadcast were printed in the newspaper format, they would not fill even one page of *The New York Times.*" (3p.105)

127

With magazines and newspapers, the content is there and it is up to the reader to choose the depth of information he/she seeks. In TV, content, scope, and sequence of items are predetermined, allowing no freedom to the viewer to skip an item and to seek more information on another. In this sense, TV news is more of a visual summary of news headlines. To really get to the news, printed news and special TV and radio news programs are the answer, as pointed out in the *Academic American Encyclopedia:*

> ...the average newspaper remains an important means by which people receive a printed record of the day's events, written for the most part in a detached manner by professionals with feeling for the reader's right to know about both the negative and positive actions of persons and groups in the public and private sectors. (1p.172)

## LOOKING INTO THE FUTURE

Prior to cable television, television channels available to a certain community were limited. Accordingly, time allocated to news programs was also limited. With the advent of cable, TV can afford to dedicate special channels for news. *Cable News Network* has been a successful venture, which success some people doubted in the beginning. Now it is a channel which broadcasts news twenty-four hours a day and is carried by all cable operators.

Other specialized channels and pay television channels carry special documentaries. *America Under Cover* is produced and broadcast by HBO and focuses on social problems, using the 60-minute magazine format.

The advancement in computer technology and telecommunications systems introduced to us the concept and the practice of information banks. With a simple personal computer keyboard, one can retrieve information from computerized information banks through telephone lines. Retrieved information can be displayed on a CRT or on the screen of a regular television set. Producing printed copies is possible if the user has access to a printer.

Teletext is another new technology in which information is sent along the regular television signals. With the help of a decoder attached to the TV set, the viewer can switch the set from running regular programs to displaying words and symbols from the teletext broadcast. Using the table of contents of the teletext, one can select news items for review. A hard copy is also possible to obtain if the user has access to a printer.

To what extent the availability of news programs on cable, satellite, and news banks can affect the network news pattern is a difficult question to answer at present. However, since networks are sensitive to what the public expects and wants, developing people's ability to intelligently view news programs and to become vocal about the advantages and shortcomings of television news is a safeguard which will enhance networks' efforts to present accurate, relevant, and unbiased news.

# REFERENCES

1. *Academic American Encyclopedia,* Vol. 14, 1985, Arete Publishing Company, Inc.

2. *Webster's New World Dictionary*

3. Lister, Walter, "News In An Entertainment Medium." in *Television Awareness Training: The Viewer's Guide For Family & Community* Ben Logan (Ed.), Abingdon/Nashville, 1979.

4. Cross, Donna Woolfold, *Mediaspeak, How Television Makes Up Your Mind,* New Jersey: A Mentor Book, New American Library, 1984.

5. Conklin, George, "Television News, News and Values" in *Television Awareness Training, The Viewer's Guide for Family and Community.* Ben Logan (Ed.), Abingdon/Nashville, 1979.

6. Chancellor, John and Walter R. Mears. *The News Business,* New Jersey: A Mentor Book, New American Library, 1983.

7. *Parade,* May 5, 1985, p.21.

# SECTION III

## ON BECOMING A CRITICAL VIEWER

Critical viewing is an outcome of planned activities in which thinking about one's relationship with television and what it offers is examined.

Chapter XIII presents critical awareness exercises for adults, and Chapter XIV reviews nationally published school critical viewing curricula.


CHAPTER XIII: ADULTS' CRITICAL VIEWING EXERCISES

CHAPTER XIV: REVIEW OF SCHOOL CRITICAL VIEWING
CURRICULA

# Chapter XIII

## ADULTS' CRITICAL VIEWING EXERCISES

*To help our children to use television in an intelligent manner, we ourselves have to use it in an intelligent manner. Before we can foster good taste in others, we have to develop that taste ourselves and believe in its necessity.*

*This chapter presents basic television awareness exercises for the adult reader.*

### Introduction:

Steps of becoming a critical viewer of television will be discussed briefly. Each step will include a worksheet, or a self-questionnaire for the reader to complete. Before answering the worksheet items, please note the chapter(s) that are recommended for reading prior to the completion of the worksheet.

It is also advisable to use the worksheets as guidelines in interviewing consenting viewers, and to share your reaction to television with them.

Seven basic steps are outlined. These steps are:

1. Understanding One's Relationship with Television
2. Understanding Television Programming Policy
3. Analyzing the Structure of News Programs
4. Analyzing Entertainment Programs
5. Analyzing Commercials
6. Collecting Information on Viewers' Interaction with Television
7. On Being an Activist

133

### Step I:  Understanding One's Relationship with TV

By definition, "critical implies an attempt at objective judging so as to determine both merits and faults." Therefore, to be a critical viewer of television does not mean finding all the mistakes of television. Primarily it means staying in control of one's television viewing. This necessitates examining one's personal relationship with television.

In an attempt to understand one's relationship with television, questions such as the following should be asked: How often do you watch television? Do you decide which programs to watch before you turn on the set? Are you willing to give up a favorite program to do something else such as reading, going for a walk, talking to a friend?

Worksheet I, **Your Personal Relationship with TV**, has a list of questions pertaining to one's relationship with TV. It is a simple tool for you to use to put on paper what you have in mind.

## Step I:   Your Personal Relationship with TV

I. The following exercise may help you in determining to what extent TV plays a part in your life.

|  | Usually | Often | Rarely | Never |
|---|---|---|---|---|
| 1. Do you automatically turn on the TV set when you get up in the morning? | ___ | ___ | ___ | ___ |
| 2. Do you automatically turn on the set the minute you come back from work? | ___ | ___ | ___ | ___ |
| 3. How often do you take your meals in front of the TV set? | ___ | ___ | ___ | ___ |
| 4. How often do you rely mainly on TV for news? | ___ | ___ | ___ | ___ |
| 5. If watching one of your favorite programs is interrupted by a social call from a friend, do you cut that call short? | ___ | ___ | ___ | ___ |
| 6. Are you a channel wanderer? (1) | ___ | ___ | ___ | ___ |
| 7. Do you keep the TV set on all the time regardless of whether or not anyone is watching? | ___ | ___ | ___ | ___ |
| 8. Do you plan your leisure time activities around your favorite programs? | ___ | ___ | ___ | ___ |

(1)  A channel wanderer turns on the set first then switches from one channel to the other until he/she finds something that looks least objectionable.

| | Usually | Often | Rarely | Never |
|---|---|---|---|---|
| 9. How often do you use TV watching to reward or to punish your children? | ____ | ____ | ____ | ____ |
| 10. How often do you ask your children not to spend too much time in front of the television set, yet you don't put a limit for yourself? | ____ | ____ | ____ | ____ |

If your answers to the previous questions tend to be in the first column, television plays a significant role in your life and you may want to re-examine your relationship with television to minimize your dependence on it.

II. The reasons I watch television are:

|  |  | Yes | No | Sometimes |
|---|---|---|---|---|
| 1. | To keep me company | ___ | ___ | ___ |
| 2. | To kill time | ___ | ___ | ___ |
| 3. | To enjoy the excitement | ___ | ___ | ___ |
| 4. | To enjoy watching my favorite actors | ___ | ___ | ___ |
| 5. | To find information I can share with my friends | ___ | ___ | ___ |
| 6. | To get information on what is happening in the world | ___ | ___ | ___ |
| 7. | To watch sports programs | ___ | ___ | ___ |
| 8. | To watch sports newscasts | ___ | ___ | ___ |
| 9. | To escape from daily life routine | ___ | ___ | ___ |
| 10. | To learn something new | ___ | ___ | ___ |
| 11. | To relax with simple material that does not necessitate mental effort | ___ | ___ | ___ |
| 12. | It is just a habit | ___ | ___ | ___ |
| 13. | (Write in) | ___ | ___ | ___ |
| 14. | (Write in) | ___ | ___ | ___ |
| 15. | (Write in) | ___ | ___ | ___ |

Based on the above, write a statement explaining why you watch TV.

III. How often do I watch television?

    Week-days    1    2    3    4    5  hours

    Week-ends    1    2    3    4    5  hours

IV. Can you turn off your set for a day or two and do something else with your free time? If the answer is yes, then by all means, do it and record the findings of your personal experience.

## Step II:   Understanding TV Programming Policy

A critical viewer should develop a clear understanding of television's programming policy. Activities recommended for this step are: (a) reading of chapter VIII, and (b) the completion of three worksheets on programming.

## Programming Exercises

For the purpose of the following exercises television programs are classified under the following types:

Adventure
Drama
Culture/Educational
Game shows
Movie
Musical
News
Police/detective/spy
Situation comedy
Soap Opera
Sports
Talk Shows
Thriller
Variety

**Worksheet 1 - Programming**

Using the TV Guide, complete the following table.
Among the channels, include a PBS Channel.

Day of the week _____

| TIME | Channel/ Program | Channel/ Program | Channel/ Program | Channel/ Program | Channel/ Program |
|---|---|---|---|---|---|
| 6:30 - 7:00 a.m. | | | | | |
| 7:00 - 7:30 a.m. | | | | | |
| 7:30 - 8:00 a.m. | | | | | |
| 8:00 - 8:30 a.m. | | | | | |
| 8:30 - 9:00 a.m. | | | | | |
| 9:00 - 9:30 a.m. | | | | | |
| 9:30 - 10:00 a.m. | | | | | |
| 10:00 - 10:30 a.m. | | | | | |
| 10:30 - 11:00 a.m. | | | | | |
| 11:00 - 11:30 a.m. | | | | | |
| 11:30 - 12:00 noon | | | | | |

*Adults' Critical Viewing Exercises*

## Worksheet II - Programming

Using the TV Guide, complete the following table.
Among the channels, include a PBS Channel.

Day of the week _____

| TIME | Channel/ Program | Channel/ Program | Channel/ Program | Channel/ Program | Channel/ Program | Channel/ Program |
|---|---|---|---|---|---|---|
| 12:00 - 12:30 p.m. | | | | | | |
| 12:30 - 1:00 p.m. | | | | | | |
| 1:00 - 1:30 p.m. | | | | | | |
| 1:30 - 2:00 p.m. | | | | | | |
| 2:00 - 2:30 p.m. | | | | | | |
| 2:30 - 3:00 p.m. | | | | | | |
| 3:00 - 3:30 p.m. | | | | | | |
| 3:30 - 4:00 p.m. | | | | | | |
| 4:00 - 4:30 p.m. | | | | | | |
| 4:30 - 5:00 p.m. | | | | | | |
| 5:00 - 5:30 p.m. | | | | | | |
| 5:30 - 6:00 p.m. | | | | | | |

**Worksheet III - Programming**

Using the <u>TV Guide</u>, complete the following table.
Among the channels, include a PBS Channel.

Day of the week _____

| TIME | Channel/ Program | Channel/ Program | Channel/ Program | Channel/ Program | Channel/ Program |
|------|---------|---------|---------|---------|---------|
| 6:00 - 6:30 p.m. | | | | | |
| 6:30 - 7:00 p.m. | | | | | |
| 7:00 - 7:30 p.m. | | | | | |
| 7:30 - 8:00 p.m. | | | | | |
| 8:00 - 8:30 p.m. | | | | | |
| 8:30 - 9:00 p.m. | | | | | |
| 9:00 - 9:30 p.m. | | | | | |
| 9:30 - 10:00 p.m. | | | | | |
| 10:00 - 10:30 p.m. | | | | | |
| 10:30 - 11:00 p.m. | | | | | |
| 11:00 - 11:30 p.m. | | | | | |

1.  Write your observations on programs telecast during the following periods:

    1.a.  6:00 a.m. to 12:00 noon

    1.b.  12:00 noon to 3:00 p.m.

    1.c.  3:00 p.m. to 7:30 p.m.

    1.d.  7:30 p.m. to 8:00 p.m. (pre-prime time)

    1.e.  8:00 p.m. to 11:00 p.m. (prime time)

2.  After studying your above findings, write a brief statement describing the following:

    2.a.  Counter programming

    2.b.  Pre-prime time programming

    2.c.  Prime time programming

3.   Repeat the same exercise on another day of the week and compare your
     results.

4.   Repeat the same exercise on a Saturday. Based on your findings, write a
     short paragraph on children's programming on Saturday mornings.

During the spring of 1985, the author asked a group of fourteen teachers to complete the preceding exercise. The following were their combined observations. You can notice how PBS offers alternatives to commercial entertainment programs. Compare your results of the preceding exercise with their results.

1.  Networks telecast similar programs during the same time slot, while independent stations counter program. In general, there are few alternative shows among commercial stations.
2.  Networks seem to use scheduling techniques to attract viewers instead of trying something unique or creative. The major networks don't take risks.
3.  Networks try to attract the majority of the audience. For instance, sports for men on Saturday afternoons, and children's cartoons on Saturday mornings. Independents sit back and take the leftovers.
4.  Except for public broadcasting, the programming of prime time consists of police/detective, situation comedy, movies, and new programs.
5.  Certain shows go into syndication. Although shows like *Barney Miller*, and *I Love Lucy* run over and over again, apparently they still do attract a fairly large audience.
6.  PBS provides programming which is consistently in contrast to all programming on other commercial channels. In addition to a variety of shows, PBS telecasts good quality documentaries.
7.  The majority of Saturday morning cartoons had the same story line: a main character - a good guy, usually accompanied by one or more minor characters - who was involved in some fight with a very obvious bad guy. The good always won over the bad.
8.  On Saturday from 5:00 to 8:00 p.m., the viewing was definitely not geared to the female audience.
9.  All of the programs, except movies, were tailored to a half-to-one hour slots. Putting a limit on the length of the program does not allow for innovative and creative programs.

**COMMENTS:**

### Step III:  Analyzing the Structure of News Programs

(Recommended reading: Chapter XII: TV NEWS)

Watch your favorite news program. Keep a paper and pencil handy to list the sequence of news stories in the program, including commercial breaks.

Repeat the same exercise on another day. Based on the information you gathered, answer the following questions:

1. How does a news program start?


2. In your opinion, what are the criteria used in selecting the lead story?


3. How many stories were presented?


4. How much time was given to international news?


5. How much time was given to national news?


6. How much time was given to local news?


7. How long was the sports section?


8. How long was the weather section?


9. How often did the newscasters carry on "happy talk" among themselves?

10. Do you think that there is more emphasis on tragic news and conflict among people?


11. How many commercial breaks were in the program?


12. How do you feel about commercials on news programs?


**General Comments:**

### Step IV:  Analyzing Entertainment Programs

(Recommended readings: Chapters VII, VIII, IX and X)

A. After viewing a situation comedy, briefly record your opinion regarding the following questions and issues.

1. What were the values the program explicitly advocated?

2. What were the values the program implied?

3. What were the men in the program like?

4. What were the women in the program like?

5. What were the children in the program like?

6. How often was sex used to exploit?

7. How often was verbal violence used as a way of evoking laughter?

8. How often was violence used? Enumerate and describe acts of violence in the program.

9. How are minorities presented in the program?

10. What did people do for a living?

11. How often were drugs and the consumption of alcohol presented as ways to soothe the troubled person?

**COMMENTS:**

B.   After viewing a police/detective program, answer the above questions. For the reader's convenience, the same questions are listed underneath.

1.   What were the values the program explicitly advocated?

2.   What were the values the program implied?

3.   What were the men in the program like?

4.   What were the women in the program like?

5.   What were the children in the program like?

6.   How often was sex used to exploit?

7.   How often was verbal violence used as a way of evoking laughter?

8.   How often was violence used? Enumerate and describe acts of violence in the program.

9.   How are minorities presented in the program?

10.  What did people do for a living?

11.  How often were drugs and the consumption of alcohol presented as ways to soothe the troubled person?

**COMMENTS:**

Repeating the same exercise with more programs will provide more data from which the reader can make an unbiased statement on the structure of situation comedy and police/detective programs.

**General Comments on Situation Comedy Programs:**

**General Comments on Police/Detective Programs:**

## Step V:   Analyzing TV Commercials

Recommended readings: Chapter XI: "TV Commercials," and
Appendix I: "Content Analysis of TV Commercials."

Six plans of television commercials have been identified:

**association**          the product is associated with a pleasant experience

**demonstration**        the product is used to show what it looks like and
                         how it functions

**informative**          the product is presented with the intention of
                         impressing the viewer with its quality

**plot**                 the product is presented as an answer to a problem

**staged**               the product is presented in a staged action showing
                         people satisfied with its use

**testimonial**          a person or persons praise the product

1.   Choose one commercial at a time. Think about its structure and see
     which one of the above plans applies to that commercial.

2.   Repeat for other commercials until you accumulate a few under each of
     the six plans.

3.   What are the messages different plans communicate?

     a. association

     b. demonstration

     c. information

     d. plot

     e. staged

     f. testimonial

4. What does the medium use to impress the viewer?

    - choice of color

    - choice of camera angles

    - acting

    - exaggerated motion

    - choice of music

    - other (consult the check list in Appendix I for more items)

5. Describe the physical appearance of major characters in the commercials.

6. Does sound appear louder than that of the program?

7. How often is the name of the product repeated?

8. To what extent is sex used to sell the product?

9. Can you think of any element in the commercial that was there for no reason?

10. What do commercials advocate in general?


11. What are the products advertised during late afternoon?


12. What are the products advertised during prime time?


13. What are the products advertised on Saturday?



Based on your observations, write a short essay on values advocated by commercials, or on children consumerism and television commercials.

### Step VI: Collecting Information on Viewers' Interaction with Television

That children are a special audience with special needs is a significant fact which critical viewers should continue to indicate. Some of the things that keep this fact fresh in our minds are observing children as they watch television, and talking with them about their television experience. Sometimes their views on television throw more light on the role of that medium in their lives.

The following is a questionnaire in two parts: *You & Your TV Set,* and *You & TV Commercials.* The questionnaire is designed for use with children 10-14 years of age. Younger children might use them; however, some children will need help in reading the questions.

# YOU AND TELEVISION

Part I. *You and Your Television Set*

Please check or circle your answers.

Name: (optional) _____     _____ Male

Grade:    _____                        _____ Female

Age:      _____

1.  How many TV sets do you have in your home?

    0     1     2     3     4     5     *more*

2.  Do you have a TV set in your room?

    *Yes*          *No*

3.  During weekdays, how many hours do you watch TV?

    *0-1 hours a day*      *1 - 2 hours*        *2 - 3 hours*

    *3 - 4 hours*          *4 or more hours*

4.  On weekends, when do you watch TV, and what time?
    (You may circle more than one.)

| | | | |
|---|---|---|---|
| *On Saturday mornings* | *6 - 8 a.m.* | *8 - 10 a.m.* | *10 - 12 noon* |
| *Saturday afternoons* | *12 - 2 p.m.* | *2 - 4 p.m.* | *4 - 6 p.m.* |
| *Saturday nights* | *6 - 7 p.m.* | *7 - 8 p.m.* | *8 - 9 p.m.* |
| | *9 - 10 p.m.* | *10 - 11 p.m.* | *11+ p.m.* |
| *On Sunday mornings* | *6 - 8 a.m.* | *8 - 10 a.m.* | *10 - 12 noon* |
| *Sunday afternoons* | *12 - 2 p.m.* | *2 - 4 p.m.* | *4 - 6 p.m.* |
| *Sunday nights* | *6 - 7 p.m.* | *7 - 8 p.m.* | *8 - 9 p.m.* |
| | *9 - 10 p.m.* | *10 - 11 p.m.* | *11+ p.m.* |

155

5.  How many hours do you watch TV on the weekend?

> *On Saturdays* —  *0 - 1    1 - 2    2 - 3    3 - 4    4 - 5    5 - 6    7+*
>
> *On Sundays* —  *0 - 1    1 - 2    2 - 3    3 - 4    4 - 5    5 - 6    7+*

6.  During the week, when do you watch TV?
        (You may circle more than one)

> *Before school    After school    Before supper    After supper*

7.  What programs do you watch on weekdays?

> *Monday*
>
>
> *Tuesday*
>
>
> *Wednesday*
>
>
> *Thursday*
>
>
> *Friday*

8.  Do you usually watch TV

> *Alone    With friends    With parents    With brothers and sisters*

9.  Do you choose all the programs you watch?

> *Never        Sometimes        Always*

156

10. Who makes the choice most often?

    *I do      My brothers or sisters      My parents      Others*

11. When watching TV with others, do you talk about what you watch?

    *Yes           No           Sometimes*

12. What kinds of programs do you watch?

    | | | | |
    |---|---|---|---|
    | Adventure shows | *Never* | *Sometimes* | *Often* |
    | Cartoons | *Never* | *Sometimes* | *Often* |
    | Sports | *Never* | *Sometimes* | *Often* |
    | Talk shows | *Never* | *Sometimes* | *Often* |
    | Movies | *Never* | *Sometimes* | *Often* |
    | News | *Never* | *Sometimes* | *Often* |
    | Soap operas | *Never* | *Sometimes* | *Often* |
    | Police, Detective shows | *Never* | *Sometimes* | *Often* |
    | Mystery shows | *Never* | *Sometimes* | *Often* |
    | Situation comedy | *Never* | *Sometimes* | *Often* |
    | Special educational programs | *Never* | *Sometimes* | *Often* |

13. Name 5 of your favorite TV programs:

    *1.* _____

    *2.* _____

    *3.* _____

    *4.* _____

    *5.* _____

157

14. What do you like about your favorite programs?
    (You may check more than one.)

    _____  *They are fun to watch.*

    _____  *They are exciting.*

    _____  *The acting is good.*

    _____  *I like the people they are about.*

    _____  *I like the actor or actors.*

    _____  *They teach me about things I want to know more about.*

    _____  *I like the action in them.*

    _____  *Colors are really great.*

    _____  *Other.*

15. What kind of programs do you think are not shown enough on TV?

    _____

    _____

16. Do you always pay attention to what's on TV?

    *Yes*              *No*              *Sometimes*

17. If you don't, why?

    _____  *I wait to see if anything good might come on.*

    _____  *It keeps me company.*

    _____  *I feel bored or restless.*

    _____  *I don't know why, I just don't.*

18. Do you munch out when you watch TV?

    *Never*              *Sometimes*              *Often*

158

19. Do you have cable TV?

    *Yes*          *No*          *I don't know*

20. Do you have a movie channel?

    *Yes*          *No*          *I don't know*

21. What are your favorite channels?


22. Do you have a video recorder?

    *Yes*          *No*          *I don't know*

23. How many hours a week do you watch programs on videotape?

    | | | |
    |---|---|---|
    | *1 - 2  a week* | *2 - 3  a week* | *3 - 4  a week* |
    | *4 - 5  a week* | *5 - 6  a week* | *6 - 7  a week* |
    | *7 - 8  a week* | *8 - 9  a week* | *9 - 10  a week* |
    | | *10+  a week* | |


**Thank you for completing Part I.**

# YOU AND TELEVISION

## Part II.   You and TV Commercials

*Please check or circle your answers.*

Name: (optional) _____ _____ Male

Grade: _____                                           _____ Female

Age:    _____


1.   What do you usually do during commercials?

    *Talk*      *Play*      *Read*      *Do homework*

  *Watch the commercial*      *Just stay there*      *Leave the room*


2.   Why do you think TV commercials are on TV?

    _____ *To pay for the program's time on the air.*

    _____ *To provide a break.*

    _____ *To tell about new products.*

    _____ *To convince you to buy the product.*


3.   Do you think TV commercials tell the truth?

    *Never*      *Sometimes*      *Often*

4.   Do you find TV commercials more interesting than programs?

    *Never*      *Sometimes*      *Often*


160

5. Can you name some specific commercials *you like*?

   *1.*

   *2.*

   *3.*

   *4.*

   *5.*

6. *You like* those commercials because . . .

   _____ *Of the music*

   _____ *Good songs*

   _____ *Beautiful scenery*

   _____ *The product advertised is interesting*

   _____ *The acting is good*

   _____ *The dialogue is funny*

   _____ *I know the actor in the commercial*

7. Do you dislike some commercials?

   *Yes*          *No*

8. Name some commercials *you don't like.*

   *1.*

   *2.*

   *3.*

   *4.*

   *5.*

9. You dislike the above commercials because . . .

_____ *The commercial is a lie.*

_____ *It is embarrassing.*

_____ *The acting is bad.*

_____ *The sound is too loud.*

_____ *I have seen it too many times.*

_____ *It is boring.*

10. Do you think most people own the products advertised on TV?

     *Yes*        *No*        *I don't know*

11. If you see a product advertised on TV and you like it, you . . .

_____ *Ask your parents to buy it.*

_____ *Go to the store to see it and try it out.*

_____ *Wish you could buy it, but forget about it.*

_____ *Save to buy it with your own money.*

12. Have you bought products because you saw them advertised on TV?

     *Never*     *Sometimes*     *Often*

13. Was it as good as it seemed on the television commercial?

     *Yes*      *No*      *It was better*

14. Do you think TV should have commercials?

     *Yes*      *No*

**Thank you for completing Part II.**

# STEP VII: ON BEING AN ACTIVIST

It is not enough to know and understand the role and effects of television on our lives. Since we are partners with the television industry in what comes on the television set - refer to Chapter II: The Critical Viewer - it becomes essential that critical viewers of television have to be activists in bringing change in the quality of the society's television experience. The following is a list of activities a critical viewer may consider.

1.  Voice your concern. You will be surprised to note how many people share the same concern.

2.  Discuss TV at home with your children to help them look at TV from a fresh point of view. That discussion can lead into family policy regarding what programs are to be watched. Turning off the set without children's understanding could have negative effects and could make television more attractive. It has been pointed out that thinking about one's relationship with television is the first step in developing children's critical viewing. Guiding them to examine their relationship with television will be more effective than turning off the set.

    Watching television with your children is an excellent opportunity to help them examine and not just absorb what they see. Through short comments, simple but direct, and intelligent questions, parents can teach children that the world of television is not *really real*.

3.  Familiarize yourself with civic, federal, and national organizations interested in improving the quality of television experience for people of all ages. (Please see Appendix II, Associations and Organizations.)

4.  Think about creative uses of television with young people. Rosemary Lee Potter's study - see Chapter 14 - showed many examples of positive uses of commercial television in teaching reading and thinking skills. *Teachers' Guides to Television* (1) is a helpful reference to locate entertaining programs that have educational value. In addition, each issue contains synopses and teaching strategies for using specially selected programs.

5.  Be instrumental in having your school system adopt critical viewing curricula. Chapter XIV summarized nationally published critical viewing curricula developed for different school levels. Some schools have developed their own TV curricula based on their needs and resources. In addition, some pioneering teachers have introduced new units into their courses on critical viewing of television.

# REFERENCES

1. *Teachers' Guides To Television*, (Semi-annual), 699 Madision Avenue, New York, N.Y. 10021.

   Other recommended resource materials on the creative use of commercial materials include:

   CBS Television Reading Program, CBS Entertainment Division, 51 West 52nd Street, New York, NY 10019; scripts and teacher guides to selected CBS TV programs.

   Prime Time School Television (PTST), 40 E. Huron St., Chicago, IL 60611; PTST is a national organization that produces and distributes teachers guides to public, commercial and cable television programs regularly throughout the school year.

# Chapter XIV

# REVIEW OF SCHOOL
# CRITICAL VIEWING CURRICULA

*Four nationally published critical viewing curricula are reviewed.
The first two are designed for elementary and junior high school
students. The third and the fourth are suitable for high school
students.*

There are few published critical viewing skills curricula. The following is
a summary, and not an evaluation, of four publications.

## SUMMARY — CRITICAL VIEWING CURRICULA

1.  *GETTING THE MOST OUT OF TELEVISION:*
    **Getting the Most Out Of Television** (1) is a curriculum designed by
    Drs. Jerome and Dorothy Singer of the Yale University Family
    Television Research Center and Diana M. Zuckerman, Radcliffe
    College, Harvard University. The target students are those in grades
    3-6, and according to the authors it can be adapted for use in grades 7
    and 8.

    The objectives of the curriculum are to help young people to:

    (1)  understand how the television medium works, from its basic
         technology to its total communication impact.

    (2)  develop vocabulary, writing, and critical thinking skills.

    (3)  explore personal and social values conveyed by television news,
         drama and documentaries.

    (4)  become discriminating consumers by learning how and why
         television commercials are made.

    (5)  distinguish between fact and fiction, fantasy and reality, actual
         and staged violence.

    Eight lessons were designed "to use children's natural interest in
    television to enhance cognitive skills. The emphasis is put on teaching
    children about television so that they can better understand the medium and
    what it offers, so that they can learn to be less passive viewers and more
    discriminating consumers." (1 p.ix)

165

The authors state the primary objectives of the eight lessons as follows:

1. To teach children how television works
2. To teach children to distinguish between reality and fantasy on television programs
3. To teach children about the purpose of commercials and the techniques used for product enhancement
4. To help children develop an understanding of themselves by discussing television characters
5. To teach children that they should not generalize about minority group members from the few examples portrayed on television
6. To teach children that the violence on television should not be imitated
7. To teach children that they can become more in touch with the world events by watching television
8. To teach children that they can get more out of television by being discriminating viewers and consumers.

The lessons were written in conjunction with seven programs available on both videotape and 16-mm films from ABC Wide World of Learning. However, the authors indicate that the lessons can be easily taught without the use of the tapes or the films. The seven programs are:

1. THE TECHNICAL SIDE OF TV, (how television pictures are made and broadcast, and what a television studio, set and control room look like.)
2. PEOPLE MAKE PROGRAMS, (the television team members who plan and produce shows)
3. THE MAGIC OF TELEVISION, (special effects, dissolves and slow motion; how one distinguishes fantasy from reality on television)
4. CHARACTERS WE SEE ON TELEVISION, (how do television characters become role models whom we imitate? How do stereotyping and fictional conventions ignore the complexities of human nature?)
5. ACTION AND VIOLENCE, (the difference between fantasy action and the real-life action of news and sports. How is TV violence staged, and why is it dangerous to imitate?)
6. THE REAL WORLD OF TELEVISION, (various forms of news programs available on television; how does television news relate to magazines, newspapers and other news formats?)

7.   COMMERCIALS, (why are commercials made, and how do they influence us? How can we become more discriminating consumers?)

For each title there is an accompanying guide and workbook.

2.   *CRITICAL TELEVISION VIEWING: A LANGUAGE SKILLS WORK-A-TEXT*

The curriculum was developed by WNET-13, the New York public television station, with funding from the U.S. Office of Education and Welfare. (2)

The curriculum defines critical viewing of television as "the ability to analyze, evaluate and express what is seen and heard on television —orally, in writing or in choice of reading materials." The target students are grades 5-9.

Two *Work-A-Text* books are available. One is designed for students, and the second one is the Teachers' Annotated Edition.

The ten chapters of *Work-A-Text* contain activities, charts, games, logs, illustrations, and photographs to introduce and reinforce basic skills and concepts. The following is a brief outline of the ten chapters and the objectives of each.

1.   How Does Television Fit into Your Life? To examine different media and the ways in which they use them so that they may begin to be aware of how the media, especially television, influence their lives.

2.   What Are The Ingredients for a Television Story? To examine television stories in terms of character, setting, conflict, plot, theme and logic so that they begin to understand the difference between television's fiction and life's reality.

3.   Who Puts a Television Program Together? To learn about some of the production elements in a TV program and to learn to read a TV script.

4.   How Do Different Types of Television Programs Compare to Each Other? To become aware of different types of television programs and their identifying characteristics so that they can become aware of why they prefer one type of program over another.

5.   How Does Television Persuade Us? To become aware of persuasion techniques on television so that they may become aware of how commercials and regular programming can affect viewers' opinions and behavior.

6. How Do You Analyze TV News? To understand the elements of TV news as it compares to other media.

7. How Does a Televison Program Get on the Air? To experience reading a TV script and become aware of how some kinds of programming decisions are made.

8. What Do You Like about the Television Program You Watch? To analyze the individual program elements and develop the skills necessary to form and support opinions of television programs.

9. How Do You Review a Television Program? To examine and organize opinions of individual program elements into a cohesive written review.

10. How Can You Become a More Critical Television Viewer? To make judicious use of television viewing time.

3. *INSIDE TELEVISION — A GUIDE TO CRITICAL VIEWING*

The guide was jointly produced by WGBH Educational Foundation, Office of Radio & Television for Learning, Boston, Massachusetts, and Far West Laboratory for Education Research and Development, San Francisco, California. (3)

*INSIDE TELEVISION* aims to teach high school students to become more sophisticated, discriminating viewiers of television, and more sophisticated, discriminating thinkers in general. It can be used as the basis for a full semester course or as a supplement to certain standard high school subjects.

The complete course is divided into the following seven units:

| Unit I | *You & Television* (An introduction to television as a medium, and to the way Americans use it) |
| Unit II | *The Television Industry* (A comprehensive explanation of television as a business, its history and regulations) |
| Unit III | *Programs and Production* (Dramatic form, characterization, production techniques) |
| Unit IV | *Selling* (Commercials, public service announcements, political advertising and packaging) |
| Unit V | *That's The Way It Is? TV News* (News and information programming) |
| Unit VI | *The Television Environment* (Television's subtle messages and the effects of viewing) |
| Unit VII | *A Saving Radiance?* (Future technology and a re-examination of the issues raised in Unit I). |

Each unit, in turn, has four interrelated components:

1. *The Text* provides information about television and its role in society.

2. *The Activities* suggest writing assignments of varying lengths, others call for a general discussion and responses to specific questions. Some activities are done individually, others are done in small groups or by the class as a whole, and some are designed as homework assignments.

3. *The Readings* encompass a variety of reprinted material. They follow the text in each unit. Assignments for readings are also given in the *Teachers' Guide.* Some of the readings entitled "In Conversation with..." are edited interviews (especially commissioned for this course) with prominent people in television including producers, directors, actors, and advertisers.

4. *The Worksheets* are provided separately and can be duplicated using copying equipment. They provide the students with the opportunity to perform a wide variety of brief written exercises for class or homework, and role-playing activities such as interviewing, scheduling programs, and writing the student's own news show.

4. *TELEVISION LITERACY: CRITICAL VIEWING SKILLS:*

*Television Literacy* was developed by the School of Public Communication at Boston University, under contract with the Department of Education. The main objective of the curriculum is to educate and sensitize the adult population to the powerful effects of television on society. (4)

The curriculum includes a text, an instructor's guide, and a student workbook. It consists of four modules. These modules are:

1. *Behind the Scenes.* This module focuses on the inner work of television: the structure, techniques, creative process, business, politics, and the effects of television.

2. *Persuasive Programming.* This module examines persuasive techniques in presenting information in commercials, public service announcements, and institutional documentaries to sell products or ideas. The basic concepts studied in this module include: appeals, effects, methods, claims, forms, structure, and research.

3. *Entertainment Programming.* This module focuses on the structure and ingredients of prime time shows, entertainment themes on television, social behavior on television, characteristics of talk, fun, and game shows on television, and television as a popular culture.

4. *Informational Programming.* This module studies the origins, and constraints of informational programming; gathering, assigning and selecting news; organizing the news; selling the news; documentaries and special news programs; and the impact of TV news.

## VIEWING TV AND STUDENTS' EDUCATIONAL GROWTH

In addition to curricula in critical viewing, there is a wealth of information on the use of the time children and young people spend in watching television to enhance their educational growth. One of the most comprehensive studies in this area is *NEW SEASON: THE POSITIVE USE OF COMMERCIAL TELEVISION WITH CHILDREN* by Rosemary Lee Potter (5). This book demonstrates creative approaches to the use of commercial television with children to help them read and think.

Rosemary Potter based her book on one basic premise: commercial television is a common denominator in every child's life and it can be used successfully in school to tie in with many curriculum areas. She believed that the negative attitude toward commercial television has been related to the commercial exploitation of television to its audience. However, on the opposite side, research studies of the 1960s, and 1970s reported high interest and comprehension when commercial television was used as a learning motivator in reading and language activities in school. She referred to a 1971 survey from Japan which indicated that the children learned words, actions and styles from various programs and even imitated these learnings through play. She further justified her point of view by referring to the fact that commercial publishers have capitalized on commercial television by marketing books, coloring books, games and activities based on television characters and programs. Based on these observations, Potter believed that it is only logical that teachers should make a use of the medium as a learning tool.

The author showed many examples of the positive learning potential of commercial television such as reluctant readers who eagerly read scripts and books related to television programs or movies with a result of increased level of verbal language skills.

The main part of the book consists of games to develop "reading and thinking skills (as well as) math, science, social studies and career education experiences." (5p.21) The games are listed alphabetically but are designated according to the level where the game was introduced — primary, intermediate, or secondary — and adaptations to other grade levels are suggested as well as the desired objective.

## EFFORTS OF INDIVIDUAL TEACHERS

Individual teachers convinced of the prominent place of television in the lives of their students and the importance of directing that influence to the betterment of the students' lives plan a variety of critical viewing experiences. For instance, a language arts teacher in a Southern Connecticut school system, designed a critical viewing unit for a special education class. One of her interesting findings is related to emotionally disturbed children who view long hours of television to substitute for the lack of peer interaction. (One of her students used to watch 60 hours a week of television.) As a result of introducing the critical viewing unit, the emotionally disturbed children found the teacher as a person with whom they can communicate on topics of interest. She felt as if she became the peer those children miss. She also found that they enjoy talking about their television experience. The discussions she had with her students were helpful to her in indicating their values and the things they like and dislike. (6)

---

Based on the degree of modern society's dependence on television for information, entertainment, and spending a large portion of leisure time, as well as on the basis of the tremendous effects that television has on every one of us, developing critical viewing skill should not be left to chance. Planned learning strategies for developing young people's critical viewing skills are a must in school curricula. This will happen only when both teachers and parents believe in its necessity, and dedicate the efforts for its implementation.

In 1935, Rudolf Arnheim, a scholar in the field of visual communication wrote:

> If we succeed in mastering the new medium (television), it will enrich us. But it can also put our minds to sleep. We must not forget that in the past the inability to transport immediate experience and to convey it to others made the use of language necessary and thus compelled the human mind to develop concepts. For in order to describe things one must draw the general from the specific; one must select, compare, think. When communication can be achieved by pointing with the finger, however, the mouth grows silent, the writing hand stops, and the mind shrinks. (7)

Comparing people who know how to observe with others, he said:

> . . . people who know how to observe and to draw conclusions from what they see will profit greatly. Others will be taken in by

171

the picture on the screen and confused by the variety of visible things. After a while they may even cease to feel confused: proud of their right to see everything and weaned from the desire to understand and to digest, they may feel great satisfaction . . . (7)

A critical viewer is a person who knows how to observe, and how to evaluate what is observed — skills needed to master the medium of television. Those skills should be practiced by parents and adults, and taught to children. And the best way of teaching those skills is by setting up models of critical viewers children can imitate.

# REFERENCES

1. Singer, D.G., et al. *Getting the Most Out of TV*, Santa Monica, California: Goodyear Publishing Co., 1981.

2. WNET, *Critical Television Viewing: A Language Skills Work-A-Text*, Student Edition and Teachers' Guide. New York: Globe Book Co., 1980.

3. White, Ned, *Inside Television: A Guide to Critical Viewing*, Palo Alto, California: Science and Behavior Books, 1980.

4. School of Public Communications, *Television Literacy: Critical Viewing Skills*, Boston, Massachusetts: Dendron Press, P.O. Box 24, Kenmore Station, 1980.

5. Potter, Rosemary Lee, *New Seasons: The Positive Use of Commercial Television with Children*, Columbus, Ohio: Charles E. Merrill Publishing Co., 1976.

6. Interview.

7. Arnheim, Rudolph, "A Forecast of Television," *Film As Art*, Los Angeles, California: University of California Press, 1957. pp.195-196.

# Appendix I

## CONTENT ANALYSIS
## OF TV COMMERCIALS

"Content Analysis of TV Commercials," was originally published in *International Journal of Instructional Media,* Vol. 5(1), 1977-78. It was based on content analysis research conducted by Dr. W. Paul Maloney, and the author. The article is reprinted in its entirety, by a special permission from Baywood/Westwood Publishing Company, to demonstrate to the reader the intricate structure of the most persuasive material on television, and to illustrate the how of analyzing television commercials. It is recommended for the reader to use the checklist in Appendix A of this article in experimenting with television commercials analysis - Step V, Chapter XIII.

**Ibrahim M. Hefzallah, Ph.D.**
**W. Paul Maloney, Ed. D.**

*Television commercials are carefully designed to sell a product. Due to their substantive effects, especially on young people, there is a need to critically analyze them to reveal their content and persuasive techniques.*

*A content analysis tool comprehensive in scope and specific to television would help reveal the intricate components of a TV commercial. In this study, the researchers aimed at developing such a tool in the form of a checklist. Application of the checklist on a selected sample of TV commercials is discussed.*

*A recommendation is made to use the checklist with junior and senior high school students in units dealing with understanding television.*

## RESEARCH OBJECTIVES

Observation of peoples' reaction to TV commercials reveals the substantive effect that some of the commercials have on the television audience, especially children and young adults. Literature on television advertising supports the same claim. If the premise that commercials are effective is accepted, it is important to become aware of their characteristics and techniques of persuasion. This partially entails a critical analysis of the television commercials to reveal their content and techniques of presentation. In this analysis, careful attention should be given to every sound and every image item of the commercial. Since commercials differ in treating their products through different persuasive techniques, there is a need for the development of a content analysis tool comprehensive in scope and specific to TV commercials. This tool should encompass every element of the commercial since, as Peter Drucker observed: "Few messages are as carefully designed and as clearly communicated as the thirty-second television commercial." (1)

The researchers aimed at developing such a tool in the form of a checklist, and using the checklist in analyzing several commercials, until every possible component was included.

# RESEARCH TECHNIQUE

## FIRST: DEVELOPMENT OF THE CHECKLIST

*Review of literature on TV advertising* — The researchers reviewed the literature on TV advertising to be more aware of persuasive techniques in TV advertising. Books such as: Paul Stevens, *I Can Sell You Anything*, Vance Packard, *The Hidden Persuaders*, Wilson Bryan, *Subliminal Seduction*, and Edward Buxton, *Promise Them Anything*, were of a particular help. (2-5)

*Review of audio-visual programs of TV advertising* — CBS Special Report, *You and The Commercials; Buy, Buy*, Churchill Films; *60 Second Spot: The Making of a TV Commercial*, Pyramid Films; and *The Consumer Game*, Pyramid Films, were very helpful in revealing the intricacies of making TV commercials.

*Screening of TV commercials* — Screening of variety of TV commercials on 16mm films which were made available to the researchers. The products in these commercials were hair spray; dishwashers; detergents; dairy products; deodorants; soap; a varitey of medical products such as: asprin, antacids medicine, cough drops, mouthwash; electronic products; soup; cereals; and cosmetic products.

A pilot checklist was developed after the first screening of the above commercials. Further screening of the same commercials helped add more items to the checklist.

*Conducting informal discussions* — Informal discussions were held with graduate students, parents, children and adolescents to determine components of TV commercials that attract their attention. The researchers conducted these discussions independently from each other then met to review their findings. A second revision of the checklist was then completed.

*Analyzing and evaluating TV commercials* — Watching commercials on TV with the objective of analyzing them and discussing their components in several meetings which the researchers conducted between themselves. A third and a last revision of the checklist was achieved. (Please see Appendix A.)

## SECOND: APPLYING THE CHECKLIST ON A SELECTED SAMPLE OF TV COMMERCIALS

*Selecting the sample*— There are many ways of selecting television commercials for testing the comprehensive and specific dimensions of the checklist. Some of these ways are: random sampling of commercials from one channel, or from the three major networks; a simultaneous recording of commercials broadcast on the three major networks and local stations during the prime hours on a weeknight; commercials on one type of product such as dairy products; those which were submitted to the CLIO (1) organization in a certain year; and, the CLIO Award Winning Commercials. After a lengthy discussion on the merits and limitations of each choice, a decision was made to select the CLIO Awards sample for the following reasons:

1. The sample covers different types of products.
2. The sample includes 30-second, 45-second, and 60-second commercials thus covering the different durations of commercials on the TV screen.
3. The sample was judged by professionals as the best commercials. Granting that the best commercials are not necessarily the most effective ones in selling a product, yet they are considered to be technically superior in their message presentation.
4. The sample was available on 16mm film which would allow its screening under different modes.
5. The sample can be made available from the CLIO Library to anyone who is interested in examining the sample used in this study.

*Applying the checklist* — The CLIO Award Winners of 1973 are in 16mm color motion picture film (see Appendix B). The film was procured from the CLIO Film Library. Each of the researchers screened the film under the following modes:

1. Uninterrupted screening of the whole film with the image projected on a 70" x 70" screen.
2. Uninterrupted screening of the whole film with the image projected on an area equivalent to that of a 23" diagonal TV screen.
3. Uninterrupted screening of the whole film through film-chain unit that produced a black and white TV picture on a 23" diagonal TV screen.
4. Screening of the individual commercials (29 commercials ranging from 30-seconds to 90-seconds):
   - A motion picture projector with freeze-frame and reverse motion was used for this purpose. The commercial was projected and reprojected until every item on the checklist was completed.
   - A film viewer was used to study the composition of some shots and to study unusual shots and optical effects frame by frame.
5. The researchers rated each of the twenty-nine commercials independently. Upon completion the researchers compared their findings. In those cases where agreement was not immediate, the commercial in question was reviewed, reanalyzed and consensus achieved.

1 The CLIO Organization was founded in 1960 to conduct the Annual CLIO Awards Competition, judged by advertising professionals. For more information write to: CLIO Awards, The American TV and Radio Commercials Festivals, 30 East 60th Street, New York, New York 10022.

# FINDINGS

## FIRST: THE CHECKLIST

The checklist was developed into four major sections. The first section, "General Information" contained four items: title of the commercial, product and sponsor, length of the commercial, and color vs. black and white.

The second section dealt with the locale in which the product was presented. These types were indoor, outdoor or no background. The time of the day was also included: daytime, nighttime or indeterminate time.

The third section dealt with the major characters. Major characters were classified under two headings: Human Beings and Animals.

Under "Human Beings" classification ten items were identified: number of characters, sex, age, relationship between characters, occupation, economic status, race, nationality, marital status, and clothing.

The age item was broken into five age brackets. Children (infant - 12 years), adolescent (13 - 19), young adults (20 - 30), middle adult (31 - 65), and senior citizen (66 - plus).

In the five items dealing with relationship between characters, occupations, economic status, nationality and marital status, three categories were identified: expressed, implied and an indeterminate status. A space for description of specifics related to these items was provided.

Under the race item four categories were identified: Caucasian, black, yellow and indeterminate. An indeterminate category would be applicable to a character with his back to the camera all the time and with the absence of any visual or audio cue to identify his race.

Under the clothing item an identification of the era: modern, past, and future was included. Then, the clothing was further identified according to six different types: casual, intimate, formal, occupational, recreational and other with a detailed description.

Under the second classification of major characters, animals, a space was left for a full description of the animals in terms of type and number.

The fourth section dealt with the *Action,* and it included three major parts: type of action, visual, and audio components of the commercial.

Under the type of action three types were identified: live, animated, and live and animated. The commercial structure or plan was identified as one of six categories: association, demonstration, informative, plot, staged and testimonial.

In analyzing the visual component nine items were identified:

1. color: realistic, exaggerated, or symbolic
2. subtitles
3. labels
4. verbal frames

5. verbal frame and picture
6. presence of unusual shots (e.g., very low or very high angles, tilted angles, etc.)
7. use of special lenses and prisms
8. actors movements natural, exaggerated, and/or emphasizing parts of the body and
9. persuading use of optical effects

In analyzing the audio component attention was given to the verbal message, sound effects and music. Under the verbal message five items were identified:

1. brand repetition
2. rate of delivery
3. mode of delivery:
   • narration and song
   • narration, song and dialogue
   • narration only
   • song only
4. voice:
   • natural human voice (sex and age level)
   • exaggerated human voice
   • impersonation: people or machine-like
5. background voices whether they were recognizable, unrecongnizable or absent

In analyzing the sound effects four categories were identified: realistic, symbolic, exaggerated, or none. The music items included these three categories: mood music, identification music, or none.

A space was provided on the checklist to transcribe the verbal message of the commercial.

## SECOND: APPLYING THE CHECKLIST TO THE CLIO AWARD SAMPLE

Applying the checklist to the CLIO sample proved that the checklist was comprehensive in scope and specific to TV commercials. Attempting to complete the checklist items helped the researchers to examine the commercial more closely. For example, in analyzing the visual component of *Del Monte Salmon* under "Labels" item, a filmviewer had to be used to study the cans of Del Monte products which were flashed on the screen. It was found that forty-four cans were shown at the speed of 2/25 of a second for each and that the name of the company fell on the same area on the screen.

Through the application of the checklist, the researchers found interesting information which they would like to share briefly with the reader.

*Length and color vs. black and white* — The most frequently employed length was 60 seconds in 59.5 percent of the sample. The 30-second length was used in 35 percent of the sample. The 45-second and the 90-second lengths were seldom used - 3.5 percent of the sample for each length.

All of the twenty-nine commercials were in color. The use of color was never exaggerated. Some commercials tended to use warm colors like the colors in 9 and 15 "Father and Son" and "Fruit." However, the overall use of color was primarily to depict people in their everyday milieu as they developed a need for, or as they used the product.

*Locale* - Analysis of the commercials' locales revealed the following:

1.  A tendency to present the product in an outdoor locale rather than in an indoor locale.
2.  Abstract locale was seldom used; only 3.5 percent of the sample was shot within an abstract locale.
3.  Identification of the locale whether outdoor or indoor was frequently practiced as found in 92.1 percent of the sample. In only 6.9 percent of the sample the subjects were shot in limbo.
4.  The majority of the commercials depicted action played against a daytime setting as 72.5 percent of the sample had daytime shots only.

*Major and type of characters* — To minimize the degree of subjectivity in analyzing the major characters first, the researchers differentiated between an implicit expression and an explicit expression of the relationship between the characters, their occupation, their economic status, their nationality and their marital status. An explicit expression is one in which the identity of the character is expressed in the narration, and an implicit expression is one in which the identity of the character is only visually portrayed. Second, the researchers viewed the commercials independent from each other, then met to discuss their findings.

Analysis of the major characters in terms of number of people, sex, age group and relationship between the characters revealed the following:

1.  The product was never presented by itself. Human beings, animals and objects were used to introduce and present the product.
2.  Human beings appeared in 93.2 percent of the commercials. In two commercials only 6.8 percent of the sample, animals — salmon and a dog — were the major characters.
3.  Males were shown more frequently than females, as eighty of the 111 major characters who appeared in the sample, or 72 percent, were males.

4. Crowds appeared in two of the commercials or in 6.8 percent. In both instances they were football audiences serving a background to the major action.
5. Middle adults, ages thirty-one through sixty-five, appeared more in TV commercials that any other age group. Adolescents and senior citizens age groups were less frequent. Young adults (31.5%) and middle adults (42.3%) constituted 73.8 percent of the major characters.
6. In commercials where a relationship between major characters was applicable, it was found that the relationship was visually implied in 58.3 percent, orally expressed in 16.5 percent, and indeterminate in 15.9 percent.
7. Animals and objects which were portrayed as characters in the commercials were considered in terms of their roles as either a major role like Sergeant's Flea Collar, *"Barney's World,"* or a supporting role as animals appeared in Coca-Cola *"Country Sunshine,"* and the following were discovered:
   - Animals played a supporting role in four commercials.
   - Objects played a major role in four commercials. In all of these, the object was the product presented in the commercials.

***Occupation and economic status of major characters —*** Analysis of the major characters in terms of their expressed or implied occupation revealed a tendency not to explicitly identify the occupations of the major characters as demonstrated in 40 percent of the sample in which the occupations were not visually or orally identified and in 56 percent of the sample, in which occupaitons were implied.

1. There was a tendency to imply the economic status of the major actors as 84 percent of the twenty-five commercials where this category was applicable, implied the economic status. In the other 16 percent, four commercials, the economic status was unidentifiable. In two of these commercials - Coca-Cola, *Raft,* and Scholl, *Stagecoach* - the setting was that of the 1800s. The third commercial - Binanca, *Put A Little Fun -* was composed from a series of head shots and no background was seen. The fourth commercial, ABC - *1972 Summer Olympics,* the players were shot while demonstrating their Olympic skills, no background was seen either.
2. The majority of the commercials, 72 percent, implied middle class economic status. One commercial, Coca-Cola, *Counselor,* implied inner city lower economic status.

***Race*** - In one commercial only, #3, one of the characters had his back to the camera and the researchers were unable to determine his race. The majority of the major characters were white as they formed 86 percent of the total number of characters. Black characters formed 10.5 percent.

*Nationality* - In twenty-three of the commercials, the nationality of the major characters was implied as American. In one commercial only, ABC-TV, "*1972 Summer Olympics*," the American nationality was orally expressed. In Datsun, Dali/Wagon, the Spanish nationality was implied.

*Marital Status* - Commercials that had exclusively male characters or objects or animals constituted thirteen commercials and were considered as nonapplicable cases. Because of its strong marital implication, commercial #9, Gillette Platinum Plus, *Father-Son*, was included in the applicable group, although it had male characters only. On that basis, it was found that in sixteen commercials where the marital category was applicable, one commercial, 6.3 percent explicitly expressed marriage, seven commercials, 43.5 percent implied marriage, and eight commercials, 50 percent marriage between the characters was indeterminate. From this analysis it can be concluded that there was a tendency to keep the marital status of the major characters indeterminate, and if the marital status of the major characters was indicated, it was implied rather that expressed.

*Clothing* - In four commerials, 4, 12, 14, 16 the clothing category was nonapplicable. From analyzing the twenty-five applicable cases it was possible to conclude the following:

a.  The sample showed present-day clothing (92%), and (8%) showed clothing from the past.
b.  One commercial, #9, (4%) showed intimate clothing.
c.  One commercial only, #13, (4%) showed two of the three major characters wearing formal clothing.
d.  Two commercials, #26 and #27 (8%) showed recreational clothing.
e.  Nine commercials (36%) showed the characters in their occupational clothing. Four of these commercials had other characters wearing casual clothing.
f.  Fifteen commercials (60%) showed the characters wearing casual clothing. From this analysis it was evident that the commericals tended to present the product in typical situation with ordinary people engaged in typical daily activities.

## TYPE OF ACTION

Analysis of the type of action used in the commercials showed that live action was used in 93 percent of the sample. This demonstrated that the emphasis was placed upon showing real people using the product. The commercial that used animation only was designed to stress the name of the product rather that the product itself. The only commercial that combined animation with live action was designed to present through the animated part how a famous artist, Salvatore Dali, interpreted the product through visual abstraction. (See Table 1.)

## THE STRUCTURAL DESIGN OR PLAN OF THE COMMERCIALS

Commercials differed in their structural designs or plans. In analyzing the sample under study six plans were revealed. These were: the *association* plan in which the product was associated with a pleasant experience; the *demonstration* plan in which the product was used to show how it looks and how it functions; the *informative* plan in which the product was presented with the intention to impress the viewer with the quality of the product; the *plot* plan in which the product was presented as an answer to a problem; the *staged* plan in which the product was presented in a staged action showing people satisfied with the product; and the *testimonial* plan in which a famous person praised the product. The distribution of the commercials according to the type of plan is shown in Table 2.

### Table 1. Type of Action

| Type of Action | Frequency | Commercial No. | Percent |
|---|---|---|---|
| Live Action | 27 | 1-23 and 26-27 | 93% |
| Animation and Live Action | 1 | 24 | 3.5% |
| Animation Only | 1 | 25 | 3.5% |
| Total | 29 | | 100% |

### Table 2. Type of Plan

| Plan Type | Number | Percent | Commercial Number |
|---|---|---|---|
| Association | 3 | 10.5% | 1,2,23 |
| Demonstration | 4 | 14% | 4,11,12,15 |
| Informative | 2 | 7% | 14,27 |
| Plot | 17 | 59.5% | 3,5-8,10,13,16,18 22,25,26,28,29 |
| Staged | 2 | 7% | 9,17 |
| Testimonial | 1 | 3.5% | 24 |

From studying this table we can conclude the following:

1. Emphasis was put upon establishing the need for a product through a plot, 59.9 percent of the sample did.
2. The demonstration plan came second on the list as 14 percent of the sample demonstrated the merits of their products.
3. The association plan was applied in 10.5 percent on the sample. There was not ample data to justify a conclusion concerning the style of the agency and producer in designing their commercials. The fact, however, that the three commercials presenting the 10.5 percent of the sample were selling one product - Coca Cola - and were produced by the same agency and same producer, should not be overlooked.
4. The informative plan was used in 7 percent of the sample.
5. The staged plan was used in 7 percent of the sample.
6. The testimonial plan was used in one commercial, 3.5 percent of the sample.

*The Plot* - From above, it was clear that more emphasis was placed upon establishing the need for a product through a plot. Sixteen plot themes were developed in the seventeen commercials employing the plot. These were:

1. Save yourself the trouble and frustations you are liable to have without the use of the product - Totes Men's Boots.
2. The dream will come true through the use of the product - "The dream of having a bank available to you anytime of the day or night to get the money that you need." First Wisconsin National Bank.
3. Save yourself the embarrassment of foot odor. Scholl Foot Powder.
4. Win with the product, it is a sure bet. Budweiser.
5. The product helps you meet your needs anywhere and at any time. Xerox.
6. Save and preserve the happy moments of your life through the use of the product. Polaroid.
7. You need the product because it is functional. Sergeant's Flea Collar.
8. If you don't do something about the problem it will hurt a dear person (that might be you). Highway Safety.
9. Practice your rights and help others regardless of their background to practice theirs, too. League of Women Voters.
10. It is fun to own and easy to use the product. (If you are middle-aged you can still enjoy life like young people.) Yamaha Motorcycles.
11. The product helps make life a little easier. McDonald's.
12. Before you become desperate use the product; it might save you lots of trouble. Rayco-Car Repair.
13. Everyone, including you, is different, yet everyone is using the product. Strauss Levi.
14. If you really need the product, use ours; it's the best. Schaefer Beer.

15. The viable uses of the product will help make life less boring to your kids. Underwood Chicken Spread.
16. Protect yourself financially by using the product. S.E. Banking Corp.

In one of the seventeen commercials having a plot plan, a humorous situation was employed. All of the commercials established a need for the product. The needs presented were personal (clothing, hygiene and identification), professional, instructional, emotional, financial, safety, political, family, transportation, pets, an enjoyable experience and relaxation.

Situations within which the need for the product was developed were realistic in all of the plot commercials except two. In the first one, #29, the idea of protecting oneself by keeping one's money in a bank was symbolized by an aggressive outburst against an employee in an office. In the second, #25, the differences between people were presented visually through animated figures synchronized with the narration.

The researchers noted a tendency in plot commercials to use half the time to present the problem and the second half to present the product and the solution to the problem.

**The Association** - Three commercials - Coca Cola, *Raft, Counselor* and *Country Sunshine* - applied the association plan. In these commercials the product was related first orally to summertime, life's good things, country sunshine, and second, visually to simple, loving and healthful surroundings. The verbal message was sung, and the slogan "It's the real thing, Coca Cola" was repeated several times. The relationship between the product and "life's good things" had no logical basis.

**The Demonstration** - Each of the four commercials that employed the demonstration plan used a different approach. These approaches were: (1) presenting the product by itself in its top performance, (2) comparing the product with a leading competitor to demonstrate visually the effectiveness of the product, (3) presenting the product in a situation where its alleged qualities were visible but not compared with other leading products, and (4) using catchy words and phrases to attract and hold the attention of the viewer while the merits of the product were demonstrated. In all of these ads, the alleged qualities of the product were demonstrated visually and reinforced orally.

**The Informative** - Two commercials - Delmonte, *Salmon*, and ABC-TV, *1972 Summer Olympics* - applied the informative plan. The information on the product was presented orally and visually. The stress was upon quality. In these commercials no attempt was made to substantiate the alleged information other than presenting a sample of the product. The food product commercial *(Salmon)* described the quality of the product using technical yet commonly understood food terminology. The terms and expressions used were: no preservatives, no artificial flavor, no food coloring, Vitamin A, Niacin, Calcium, and protein. These terms constituted 28 percent of the narration. Excluding the producer's slogan, these terms totaled 36 percent of the words used in the product's information. The *1972 Summer Olympics* (ABC-TV) emphasized the visual element in presenting a sample of its product. The fact that this commercial won the CLIO award for film effects should not be overlooked. Yet, the narration still claimed special merits of the product, "the finest television sports team in the world," and "up close and personal, the ABC way."

*The Staged* - Two commercials - Gillette Platinum Plus, *Father/Son*, and Binaca, *"Put a Little Fun"* - used the staged plan. In these commercials an action was staged where people were seen using the product to achieve a certain goal (smooth shave; a clean, fresh breath). The satisfaction with the product was expressed orally, and through pantomime.

*The Testimonal* - The testimonial plan was used least often. It was applied in one commercial only (Datsun, *Dali/Wagon*). In this commercial, a noted artist, Salvatore Dali, was commissioned to introduce the new car. He was asked to paint a portrait of the car. His oral comment about the car was "absolutely original, different, sensational." A painting, apparently by Dali, was used to introduce the car visually. The painting was abstract where the idea of originality, difference and sensation were supposed to be expressed. The car was introduced after the portrait. The artist was seen in the car and around it in a series of still shots. The implication that the car belonged to Dali was made through a shot of the artist as he opened the tailgate and picked up a painting easel and started to leave.

The testimony in this ad was given both orally and visually. Animation of this product personalized the car, and the use of selected angles made the car look longer and roomier.

## THE AUDIO COMPONENT

*Brand repetition* - Brand repitition is defined as the number of times the product's name was orally repeated in the commercial.

1. Of the twenty-nine commercials, nine or 31.5 percent repeated the brand name twice.
2. Eight of the commercials, 28 percent, repeated the brand name three times.
3. Only one commercial, 3.5 percent, did not mention the brand name in the audio component and relied upon the visual presentation for its emphasis.
4. Only two commercials, 7 percent, repeated the brand name seven times, thus relying upon the audio presentation for emphasis.

From the above it was possible to conclude that there was tendency to repeat the brand name from two to three times.

*Rate of delivery* - Analysis of the number of words in the audio component of the commercial showed that:

1.  In the 60-second commercials the average number of words used was 96.7 with a range from 27 to 165.
2.  In the 30-second commercials the average number of words was 52.8 with a range from 39 to 85.
3.  The 45-second and 90-second commercials used almost exactly the same number of words, 74 or 75.

From this analysis, the most frequently used rate of delivery was ninety words per minute.

*Mode of delivery* - The audio delivery was analyzed in each commercial to determine the mode employed according to the following criteria: narration and song; narration, song, dialogue; narration only; song only. It was found that:

1.  The overwhelming majority of the commercials employed a narrator.
2.  In narrated commercials males served more frequently as narrators than women.
3.  The most frequently employed mode of narration was the off-screen mode.
4.  Five commercials only, 17.5 percent, employed an integrated mode of delivery. In this mode the oral message was delivered through off-screen narration, a song, and a dialogue between the major characters.
5.  Narration only as a mode of delivery was employed in 45.5 percent of the sample.
6.  In five commercials only, 17.5 percent of the sample, the oral message was delivered through a song only.

*Sound effects* - Sound effects employed in the commercials were analyzed according to the following criteria: realistic, symbolic, or none. It was found that the commercials were equally divided between using no sound effects or realistic sound effects.

*Background voices* - Voices heard in the background were analyzed according to the following criteria: recognizable, unrecognizable, and none. The analysis showed that twenty-six commercials did not employ background voices, and three commercials employed recognizable voices, none of the commercials emloyed unrecognizable voices.

From this analysis it was possible to conclude that the thrust of the commericals seemed to be to provide minimal extraneous stimuli which may inhibit the overall presentation or limit its effectiveness.

*Music* - Analysis of the music employed in the commercials was done according to three criteria: mood, identification, and none. Mood music is music used to contribute to the structure and the setting of the commercial. Identification music is the music that an average viewer can associate with a certain product, such as Coca-Cola, Budweiser, McDonald commercials. The analysis showed that 49 percent of the sample employed mood music, 35 percent of the sample did not employ music, and 17.5 percent employed an established music score for the product.

From this analysis we can conclude that commercials tended to employ music as it contributes to the structure or setting of the commercials, or the identification of the product.

## SUMMARY AND CONCLUSION

Television commercials are carefully designed to sell a product. Due to their substantive effects on the television audience, especially children and young adults, there is a need to critically analyze them to reveal their content and persuasion techniques. A content analysis tool in the form of a checklist is thought to be helpful in studying the intricate components of a TV commercial. The researchers aimed at developing a content analysis checklist comprehensive in scope and specific to TV commercials, and using the checklist in analyzing several commercials to test its effectiveness.

The checklist was developed after critical study of several TV commercials. When the checklist was considered to be complete it was used in content analysis of the CLIO Awards Winner of 1973. Applying the checklist to the CLIO sample proved that the checklist was comprehensive in scope and specific to TV commercials. Attempting to complete the checklist items helped the researchers to examine the commercials more closely. The researchers recommend the use of this checklist with junior and senior high school students in units dealing with understanding television to help make them aware of the intricate design and both overt and covert intentions of the advertiser.

## APPENDIX A

Items of the Checklist Used in Content Analysis of the TV Commercials

### I. GENERAL INFORMATION

Title           Product & Sponsor

Length         Color                    B&W

## II. LOCALE

Indoor: daytime
    nighttime
    indeterminate
No Background

Outdoor: daytime
    nighttime
    indeterminate

## III. MAJOR CHARACTERS

A.   Human Beings
    1. one person
      two persons
      more than two
      crowd (24)

    2. Sex: male female

    3. Age:
      children (infant - 12 years)
      adolescent (13 - 19)
      young adult (20 - 30)
      middle adult (31 - 65)
      senior citizen (66)

    4. Relationship between major
      characters:
      expressed
      implied
      indeterminate

    5. Occupation:
      expressed
      implied
      indeterminate

    6. Economic Status:
      expressed
      implied
      indeterminate

    7. Race:
      Caucasian
      Black
      Yellow
      Indeterminate

    8. Nationality:
      expressed
      implied
      indeterminate

    9. Marital Status:
      expressed
      implied
      indeterminate

    10. Clothing:
      present past future
      casual, intimate, formal,
      occupational,
      recreational, other

B.   Animals & Objects
    major role       supporting role

## IV. ACTION

1. Type: Live Action    Animation    Live & Animation

2. Plan: Association Demonstration Information Plot Staged
   Testimony

3. Analysis:
   A. Visual Component
      1. Color: realistic exaggerated symbolic
      2. Subtitles
      3. Labels
      4. Verbal Frame
      5. Verbal Frame & Picture
      6. Presence of unusual shots
      7. Use of special lenses, prisms, etc.
      8. Actors Movements: natural exaggerated
         emphasizing parts of the body
      9. Persuading use of optical effects

   B. Audio Component
      1. Oral:
         a. Brand Repetition
         b. Rate of Delivery
         c. Mode of Delivery
            narration & song      narration, song & dialogue
            narration only      song only
         d. Voice:
            natural human voice
            impersonation: people    machine-like
         e. Background Voices:
            recognizable
            unrecognizable
            none
      2. Sound Effects: realistic
                        symbolic
                        exaggerated
                        none
      3. Music: mood
                identification
                none

The Verbal Message:

Comments:

## APPENDIX B

The CLIO Sample

| Number | Product & Title |
|--------|-----------------|
| 1 | Coca-Cola "Raft" |
| 2 | Coca-Cola "Counselor" |
| 3 | Totes Men's Boots "Puddles" |
| 4 | Mercedes Benz "Ballet" |
| 5 | 1st Wisc. Nat'l Bank "Texan/Teller" |
| 6 | Scholl Foot Powder "Stagecoach" |
| 7 | Budweiser "Five Kings" |
| 8 | Xerox "Stadium Football" |
| 9 | Gillette Platinum Plus "Father/Son" |
| 10 | Polaroid Square Shooter "Bus Stop" |
| 11 | Oxite Carpets "Zoo" |
| 12 | De-Haze "De-Fogs" |
| 13 | Blue Cross/Shield/NE Ohio "Vision Care" |
| 14 | Del Monte Foods "Salmon" |
| 15 | Bic Banana Pens "Fruit" |
| 16 | Sergeant's Flea Collar "Barney's World" |
| 17 | Binaca "Put a Little Fun" |
| 18 | Highway Safety "Beach" |
| 19 | League of Women Voters "Vote 72" |
| 20 | Yamaha Motorcycles "Birthday" |
| 21 | McDonald's "Lonely Mom" |
| 22 | Rayco "The Cliff" |
| 23 | Coca-Cola "Country Sunshine" |
| 24 | Datsun "Dali-Wagon" |
| 25 | Levi Strauss "Different The Same" |
| 26 | Schaefer "Bicycling" |
| 27 | ABC-TV "1972 Summer Olympics" |
| 28 | Underwood Chicken Spread "Spokesman" |
| 29 | S.E. Banking Corp. "Tacking" |

# REFERENCES

1. Youngblood, G., *Expanded Cinema*, New York: E.P. Dutton & Co., 1970.
2. Stevens, P., *I Can Sell You Anything*, New York: Peter H. Wyden, Inc., 1972.
3. Packard, V., *The Hidden Persuaders*, New York: David McKay Company, Inc., 1974.
4. Key, W. B., *Subliminal Seduction*, New York: New American Library, 1974.
5. Buxton, E., *Promise Them Anything*, New York: Warner Books, 1973.

# Appendix II

## ASSOCIATIONS
## AND ORGANIZATIONS

*Critical viewers realize that they are partners with the television industry in what comes on the television set. Accordingly, they recognize their role as activists in bringing change in the quality of the society's television experience. Appendix II lists organizations and associations which the reader might want to contact either to gain more information on television, or to express his/her concern.*

### NETWORKS AND LOCAL STATIONS

Letters about programming and advertising can be addressed to the presidents of the networks, or to the presidents of the local stations. *Broadcasting Cablecasting Yearbook* lists all of the television stations in operation in the U.S.A., their affiliation, addresses, and the names of the chief executive officers.

To express your concern regarding inaccurate, misleading, or potentially harmful commercials, you can write to the Federal Trade Commision, Bureau of Consumer Protection, Pennsylvania Avenue and Sixth Street, N.W., Washington DC 20580.

### ASSOCIATIONS AND ORGANIZATIONS:

**Action for Children's Television**
46 Austin Street, Newtonville, MA 02160
ACT is a citizen action group to improve children's television programming and advertising. It encourages diversity and eliminates commercial abuses from children's television. Some of its services are: a newsletter, campaigns, research information, film, and library facilities. (1,p.195)

**Children's Television Workshop**
One Lincoln Plaza, New York, N.Y. 10023
CTW is an independent, non-profit corporation that produces educational television programs for the airing on public television stations. Some of its well-known programs are *Sesame Street, The Electric Company,* and *3-2-1 Contact.*

## Corporation for Public Broadcasting (CPB)
1111 16th St. NW, Washington DC 20554
CPB is a private, non-profit corporation established by the Public Broadcasting Act of 1967. It aims at developing non-commercial television and radio services for the public. It supports stations operations and funds radio and television programs for national distribution. "CPB by means of a broad range of activities, sets national policy that will most effectively make noncommercial radio and television and other telecommunications services available to all citizens of the United States." (2,p.116)
Publications: *CPB Report; Annual Report; CPB Public Broadcasting Directory.*

## Federal Communications Commission (FCC)
1919 M St. NW, Washington DC 20554
FCC regulates radio, television, telephone, and telegraph operations within the U.S. It allocates frequencies and channels for different types of communications activities. The FCC Cable Television Bureau develops and administers policies and programs with respect to the regulation of cable television systems and related private radio facilities. (2,p.123)

## Media Action Research Center (MARC)
475 Riverside Drive, Suite 1370, New York, NY 10115
MARC is an independent, non-profit organization. Its work is made possible by grants and individual contribution. The Center was established in 1974 with a grant from the United Methodist Church. Its purposes are to: study the impact of television on viewers; publish information on television influence; help viewers develop strategies for more intentional, selective, questioning approaches to viewing through workshops and other events; and help bring about positive changes in the television system. (3,p.269)

## National Association for Better Broadcasting (NABB)
7918 Naylor Ave., Los Angeles, CA 90045
NABB promotes the public interest in broadcasting through the development of greater awareness of the public's rights and responsibilities in broadcasting. Publications: *Better Radio and Television;* and *You Own More Than Your Set.* (2,p.131)

## National Association of Broadcasters (NAB)
1771 N St. NW, Washington DC 20036
NAB is a trade association representing radio and television stations and networks. One of its objectives is to strengthen the standards of the industry, and to encourage the development of broadcasting arts.
Publications: *NAB Highlights; Radioactive.* (2,p.132)

**National Council of the Churches of Christ — Communications Commission**
475 Riverside Dr., New York, NY 10015
The Council is an ecumenical agency for cooperative work of nineteen Protestant and Orthodox denominations and agencies in broadcasting, film, cable, and print media. Its services include: liaison to network television and radio programming; film sales and rentals; distribution of information about syndicated religious programming; syndication of some programming; news and information to broadcast news media regarding work of the National Council of Churches, related denominations, and agencies; and cable television and emerging technologies information services. (2,p.134)

**National PTA**
700 N. Rush St., Chicago, IL 60611
The association is dedicated to the improvement of the quality of children's life through school, home, community, and place of worship. It has several media-related activities, one of which is a publication entitled: *Children and Television.* (2,p.136)

**PBS Video**
475 L'Enfant Plaza SW, Washington DC 20024
PBS Video markets and distributes PBS programs to schools and other institutions.

**Prime Time School Television (PTST)**
40 E. Huron St., Chicago, IL 60611
PTST produces program guides for quality commercial television programs, and periodic curriculum projects based on quality commercial, public, and cable television programs.

**Public Broadcasting Service (PBS)**
475 L'Enfant Plaza SW, Washington DC 20024
PBS serves as a distributor of national television programming which it obtains from public television stations or independent producers. Funds for technical distribution (through satellite transmission) is supplied in part by the Corportion for Public Broadcasting (CPB). Other services include national promotion, program acquisition and scheduling, legal services, development and fund-raising support, engineering and technical studies, and research. (2,p.141)

**Public Television Library (PTL)**
475 L'Enfant Plaza SW, Washington DC 20034
PTL is a rental and sales outlet for PBS productions available to individuals and organizations.
Publication: *PTL Catalog.* (2,p.141)

**Television Information Office (TIO)**
745 5th Ave., New York, NY 10022
TIO provides an information service to educators, students, government agencies, the press, the clergy, librarians, allied communications professionals, the public, and the broadcasters. "Library includes five thousand volumes, ninety-thousand documents, and information-retrieval equipment." (2,p.146) Publications include pamphlets; speeches; and paperbacks.

# REFERENCES

1. Kaye, Evelyn, *The ACT Guide to Children's Televison: Or How to Treat TV with T.L.C.* (Rev. Ed.), Boston Massachusetts: Beacon Press, 1979.

2. Miller, Elwood E. (Ed.), *Educational Media and Technology Yearbook,* Volume 11, Littleton, Colorado: Libraries Unlimited, Inc., 1985. (N.B. The author consulted a variety of reference tools in the development of the list of organizations and associations. The *Yearbook* was of special help in developing the above list.)

3. Logan, Ben (Ed.), *Television Awareness Training: A Viewer's Guide for Family and Community,* Abingdon/Nashville, 1979.

# INDEX

# THE AUTHOR

Ibrahim Michail Hefzallah has been on the faculty of Fairfield University since 1968. At present, he is a professor of educational media and director of the Fairfield University Media Center. In 1959, he received his Ph.D. from Ohio State University in educational media under the advisorship of Dr. Edgar Dale. Since then he has been engaged in teaching, research, and writing. He has published several articles on the subjects of media and television, and co-authored three Arabic texbooks in the areas of television, curriculum planning, and learning and communications media. His articles have appeared in such publications as *Babel; The National Association of Secondary School Principals Bulletin; Educational and Industrial Television (EITV); International Journal of Instructional Media; Journal of Advertising Research; The Journal of the University Film Producers Association;* and *Vocational Guidance Quarterly.* Some of his research has focused on children's viewing patterns of television, extra-curricular reading of high school students, and content analysis of television commercials.

In addition to teaching, research, and writing, the author is a producer/ director of educational and cultural television programs. A sample of programs he produced, and shown on Connecticut Public Television, includes *The Fairfield Gallery, Photographic Vision, Transcribing Jazz, Teaching Children About Families,* and *Design for Life. Design for Life* focused on teen-age smoking, and received the American Cancer Society 1980 Connecticut Media Award.

In this book he approaches the topic of critical viewing from his varied experience in teaching, media research, and television production.